PUBLIC POLICY IN AN
UNCERTAIN WORLD

PUBLIC POLICY IN AN UNCERTAIN WORLD:

Analysis and Decisions

CHARLES F. MANSKI

HARVARD UNIVERSITY PRESS

Cambridge, Massachusetts

London, England

2013

Library of Congress Cataloging-in-Publication Data

Manski, Charles F.
Public policy in an uncertain world : analysis and decisions / Charles F. Manski.
p. cm.
Includes bibliographical references and index.
ISBN 978-0-674-06689-2 (alk. paper)
1. Policy sciences. 2. Public administration. 3. Decision making.
4. Political planning—Evaluation. I. Title.
H97.M368 2013
320.6—dc23   2012014822

for the people

Contents

Preface   xiii

Introduction   1
    Rumsfeld and the Limits to Knowledge   1
    Using Policy Analysis to Inform Decisions   2
    Organization of the Book   4

I   POLICY ANALYSIS

   1   Policy Analysis with Incredible Certitude   11
       1.1   The Logic and Credibility of Policy Analysis   11
       1.2   Incentives for Certitude   13
           Support for Certitude in Philosophy of Science
       1.3   Conventional Certitudes   15
           CBO Scoring of Pending Legislation
               Scoring the Patient Protection and Affordable Care Act of 2010;
                 Credible Interval Scoring; Can Congress Cope with Uncertainty?
           British Norms
       1.4   Dueling Certitudes   23
           The RAND and IDA Reports on Illegal Drug Policy
           The National Research Council Assessment
       1.5   Conflating Science and Advocacy   27
           Friedman and Educational Vouchers
       1.6   Wishful Extrapolation   30
           Selective Incapacitation

Extrapolation from Randomized Experiments: The FDA Drug
Approval Process

*The Study Population and the Population of Interest;
The Experimental Treatments and the Treatments of Interest; The
Outcomes Measured in Experiments and the Outcomes of
Interest; The FDA and Conventional Certitude*

Campbell and the Primacy of Internal Validity

1.7   Illogical Certitude   37

Heritability

*What Does "More Important" Mean?; Heritability and Social Policy;
Gene Measurement*

1.8   Media Overreach   44

"The Case for $320,000 Kindergarten Teachers"

Peer Review and Credible Reporting

2   Predicting Policy Outcomes   47

2.1   Deterrence and the Death Penalty   48

Estimates Using Data on Homicide Rates across States and Years

2.2   Analysis of Treatment Response   51

Statistical Inference and Identification

2.3   Predicting Outcomes under Policies That Mandate a
Treatment   53

Sentencing and Recidivism

*Background; Our Analysis; Analysis Assuming Individualistic
Treatment Response; Numerical Findings; Choosing a Policy*

2.4   Identical Treatment Units   59

Before-and-After Studies

Difference-in-Differences Studies

Employment in Fast-Food Restaurants and the Minimum Wage

2.5   Identical Treatment Groups   63

Experiments with Random Assignment of Treatments

The "Gold Standard"

2.6   Randomized Experiments in Practice   67

Extrapolation

Compliance

*The Illinois Unemployment Insurance Experiment; Random
Compliance; Intention-to-Treat*

The Mixing Problem

Extrapolation from the Perry Preschool Project

Social Interactions

Local and Global Interactions
Credible Analysis of Experimental Data
2.7 Random Treatment Choice in Observational Studies   77
Rational Treatment Choice and Selection Bias
Outcome Optimization with Perfect Foresight
Regression Discontinuity Analysis
2.8 Modeling Rational Treatment Choice   81
Outcome Optimization as a Model of Sentencing
Distributional Assumptions

3 Predicting Behavior   85
3.1 Income Taxation and Labor Supply   86
The Theory of Labor Supply
Empirical Analysis
Basic Revealed-Preference Analysis
Illustration: Labor Supply under Progressive and Proportional Taxes
3.2 Discrete Choice Analysis   93
*Random Utility Model Representation of Behavior; Attribute
Representation of Alternatives and Decision Makers; Analysis with
Incomplete Attribute Data; Practicality*
College Choice in America
*Predicting the Enrollment Effects of Student Aid Policy; Power and
Price of the Analysis*
Discrete Choice Analysis Today
3.3 Predicting Behavior under Uncertainty   99
How Do Youth Infer the Returns to Schooling?
How Do Potential Criminals Perceive Sanctions Regimes?
Measuring Expectations
Pill, Patch, or Shot?
3.4 Perspectives on Rational Choice   102
As-If Rationality
Bounded Rationality
Biases and Heuristics
Widespread Irrationality or Occasional Cognitive Illusions?
The Common Thread Is Certitude

II POLICY DECISIONS

4 Planning with Partial Knowledge   115
4.1 Treating X-Pox   116

4.2   Elements of Decision Theory   116
        States of Nature
        The Welfare Function
        Welfare Functions in Studies of Optimal Income Taxation
            The Mirrlees Study
4.3   Decision Criteria   121
        Elimination of Dominated Actions
        Weighting States and the Expected Welfare Criterion
        Criteria for Decision Making under Ambiguity
            Maximin; Minimax Regret
        Using Different Criteria to Treat X-Pox
4.4   Search Profiling with Partial Knowledge of Deterrence   125
4.5   Vaccination with Partial Knowledge of Effectiveness   127
        Background
        Internal and External Effectiveness
        The Planning Problem
        Partial Knowledge of External Effectiveness
        Choosing a Vaccination Rate
4.6   Rational and Reasonable Decision Making   131
        The Savage Argument for Consistency
        Axiomatic Rationality and Actualist Rationality
        Axiomatic and Actualist Perspectives on Subjective Probability
            Ellsberg on Ambiguity
        The Quest for Rationality and the Search for Certitude

5   Diversified Treatment Choice   139
        Diversification and Profiling
5.1   Allocating a Population to Two Treatments   141
        The Welfare Function
        A Status Quo Treatment and an Innovation
            *Expected Welfare; Maximin; Minimax Regret; Choosing Sentences for
            Convicted Juvenile Offenders; Allocation of Wealth to a Safe and
            Risky Investment*
        Risk-Averse Planning
5.2   Diversification and Equal Treatment of Equals   148
        Ex Ante and *Ex Post* Equal Treatment
        Combining Consequentialism and Deontological Ethics
5.3   Adaptive Diversification   150
        Adaptive Minimax Regret
            Implementation in Centralized Health Care Systems

The AMR Criterion and the Practice of Randomized Clinical
Trials

*Fraction of the Population Receiving the Innovation; Group Subject to
Randomization; Measurement of Outcomes*

5.4   Diversification across Time or Space   154

Diversification by Cohort

Laboratories of Democracy

5.5   Adaptive Partial Drug Approval   156

The Present Approval Process

Binary versus Partial Approval

Adaptive Partial Licensing

5.6   Collective Decision Processes   160

Majority-Rule Voting with Single-Peaked Preferences

The Credibility of Single-Peaked Preferences

Strategic Interactions

Learning and Heterogeneity of Policy Preferences

Bilateral Negotiations

*Pareto Optimal Allocations; Incentive-Compatible Processes; Teacher
Evaluation in New York City*

5.7   Laissez-Faire   169

Social Learning from Private Experiences

Laissez-Faire Learning and Adaptive Diversification

6   Policy Analysis and Decisions   173

Institutional Separation of Analysis and Decisions

Doing Better

Appendix A: Derivations for Criteria to Treat X-Pox   177

Appendix B: The Minimax-Regret Allocation to a Status Quo Treatment and
an Innovation   179

Appendix C: Treatment Choice with Partial Knowledge of Response to Both
Treatments   181

References   183

Index   193

Preface

When colleagues have asked me about my work in progress over the past several years, I have described my ongoing research and then told them that the most difficult challenge I was facing was my determination to write a book in English. They often looked at me in bewilderment at this odd statement. I then explained that I was writing a book for a broad audience and that this required minimization of technical jargon and an almost complete avoidance of mathematics. I said that our society needs to face up to the uncertainties that attend policy formation. Having devoted much of the past twenty years to the development of methods for credible policy analysis and decision making, I observed that my ideas had matured to the point where they warrant the attention of citizens beyond the community of social scientists.

I have endeavored, and I hope that the result is worth the effort. It has again been a pleasure to work with Mike Aronson at Harvard University Press, who has shown faith in this project from start to finish. I am grateful to Matt Masten, John Pepper, and to anonymous reviewers for their comments on a draft of the manuscript. I am also grateful to the National Science Foundation for its financial support through grant SES-0911181.

PUBLIC POLICY IN AN
UNCERTAIN WORLD

Introduction

Rumsfeld and the Limits to Knowledge

In recent times, Donald Rumsfeld has personified the difficulty of making public policy in an uncertain world. Rumsfeld served in many capacities in the federal government, culminating in a controversial tenure as secretary of defense from 2001 to 2006. He was often forthright about the limits to knowledge, but he may be remembered for a highly inaccurate prediction of a major policy outcome.

Rumsfeld's appreciation of the limits to knowledge is evident in the "Rumsfeld's Rules" that circulated among public officials in Washington for many years. One was "Learn to say 'I don't know.' If used when appropriate, it will be often" (see Rumsfeld 2001).

In early 2002, Secretary of Defense Rumsfeld made what may be a lasting contribution to epistemology in response to a question about Iraq at a press conference. The question and response were as follows (U.S. Department of Defense 2002):

> *Question:* Could I follow up, Mr. Secretary, on what you just said, please? In regard to Iraq weapons of mass destruction and terrorists, is there any evidence to indicate that Iraq has attempted to or is willing to supply terrorists with weapons of mass destruction? Because there are reports that there is no evidence of a direct link between Baghdad and some of these terrorist organizations.

Rumsfeld: Reports that say that something hasn't happened are always interesting to me, because as we know, there are known knowns; there are things we know we know. We also know there are known unknowns; that is to say we know there are some things we do not know. But there are also unknown unknowns—the ones we don't know we don't know. And if one looks throughout the history of our country and other free countries, it is the latter category that tend to be the difficult ones.

Rumsfeld was not the first to distinguish "known unknowns" from "unknown unknowns," but he drew the distinction perceptively and in the context of an important policy matter.

Yet later in 2002, Rumsfeld felt confident enough to make what became an infamous prediction of the length of the contemplated future war in Iraq, stating (Rumsfeld 2002): "I can't tell you if the use of force in Iraq today will last five days, five weeks or five months, but it won't last any longer than that." Rumsfeld expressed some uncertainty about the length of the war. However, as we now know, his upper bound would have been too low even if he had extended it from five months to five years.

Using Policy Analysis to Inform Decisions

As Rumsfeld did regarding the length of the Iraq War, politicians routinely express certitude that policies they advocate will have favorable outcomes. They rarely provide supporting evidence, but they sometimes cite congenial findings reported by academic researchers or by analysts in government agencies or private think tanks. It is common for advocates of particular policies to assert that "research has shown" these policies to be desirable.

A reader might expect that, as an economist concerned with public policy, I would applaud the use of research findings to support policy choice. I do applaud it when the logic of the research is sound and the maintained assumptions are credible. Then the research truly informs policy making.

However, researchers regularly express certitude about the consequences of alternative decisions. Exact predictions of outcomes are common, and expressions of uncertainty are rare. Yet policy predictions often are fragile. Conclusions may rest on critical unsupported assumptions or on leaps of logic. Then the certitude of policy analysis is not credible.

I hope to move policy analysis away from incredible certitude and toward honest portrayal of partial knowledge. In a series of methodological studies (Manski 1990 and following), I have cautioned against the use of incredibly strong assumptions when performing analysis and recommending decisions. I have urged analysts to instead ask what can be learned when available data are combined with credible assumptions. The results typically are interval predictions of policy outcomes. I have shown how the form of the interval depends on the data and the assumptions. I have shown how reasonable policy choices may be made with partial knowledge of policy outcomes. I have stressed that when one has partial knowledge of policy outcomes, it may be reasonable to choose a policy that could not be optimal if one were to have complete knowledge.

I have developed this methodological research program in numerous professional journal articles and have exposited it to academic audiences in several books (Manski 1995, 2003, 2005a, 2007a) and a review article (Manski 2011a). As the program has matured, I have increasingly felt that it warrants the attention of a broader audience than those willing and able to read technical material. Hence, I decided to write this book.

Ideally, I would like the book to inform a wide spectrum of persons who typically do not have the mathematical background of academic economists. I am thinking of undergraduate and master's students in public policy and social science programs. I am thinking of the civil servants who commission, perform, or apply policy analysis. I am thinking of the government officials who make policy decisions. I am thinking of the journalists who describe and interpret policy to the public. And I am thinking of citizens who want to think deeply about policy choice.

Writing a serious book accessible to this broad audience is a challenge. The book is almost entirely "in English," meaning that I strive throughout to explain ideas in words without resort to mathematics. There are only occasional places where I decided that a bit of elementary logic or algebra could usefully sharpen the verbal exposition. To show the practical import of the material, I discuss a wide array of policy issues—from the death penalty and income taxation to drug approval and vaccination.

I expect that the ideas developed here will be clear to readers who have absorbed the major themes (not the technical details) of basic undergraduate courses in microeconomics and probabilistic reasoning. I hope that readers who do not possess this background will grasp my explanations of concepts and methods. I am aware that the task is harder when one is seeing ideas for the first time, but I know from experience that initially unfamiliar concepts can become transparent with contemplation. In any case, I intend the book for thoughtful readers who will take the time to read the material carefully. This is not a pop social science book meant for casual readers browsing an airport bookstore.

Organization of the Book

Part I, comprising Chapters 1 through 3, describes the practice of policy analysis and the inferential problems that researchers confront. I argue that credible analysis typically yields interval rather than point predictions of policy outcomes. Part II, comprising Chapters 4 through 6, examines how governments might reasonably make policy decisions when they only have partial knowledge of policy outcomes.

Chapter 1, which is based largely on one of my published articles (Manski 2011b), documents the tendency of researchers to use incredibly strong assumptions to obtain strong findings about policy. I call attention to and give illustrations of six practices that contribute to incredible certitude: conventional certitude, dueling certitudes, conflating science and advocacy, wishful extrapolation, illogical certitude, and media overreach. The chapter explains what I do not like about the current practice of policy analysis; but it is not enough to criticize. I must suggest a constructive alternative. This is the task of all that follows.

In an ideal world, persons who are not expert in research methodology would be able to trust the conclusions of policy analysis. However, the practices described in Chapter 1 indicate that consumers of policy analysis cannot safely trust the experts. Thus, civil servants, journalists, and concerned citizens need to understand prediction methods well enough to be able to assess reported findings. With this in mind, Chapters 2 and 3 describe various conventional approaches that use strong assumptions to obtain strong conclusions. I additionally describe approaches that I have developed, which use weaker assumptions to obtain interval predictions.

Chapter 2 examines the basic inferential problem that makes it difficult to predict policy outcomes. This is the absence of data on *counterfactual* outcomes—that is, the outcomes of policies that have not been implemented. I introduce the broad subject of analysis of treatment response. I then consider a relatively simple setting in which a researcher observes the outcomes experienced by members of a study population, some of whom receive one treatment and the remainder who receive another treatment. The objective is to predict the outcomes that would occur under a proposed policy mandating that everyone receive the same treatment.

I describe how researchers combine data on outcomes in the study population with assumptions of identical treatment response to predict the outcomes of such policies. Some assumptions suppose that different persons respond identically to treatment. Others assume that different groups of persons have identical patterns of treatment response. The latter idea motivates performance of randomized experiments.

To illustrate analysis of treatment response, I discuss research that aims to learn various treatment effects. I describe analysis of the deterrent effect of the death penalty on homicide, the effect of sentencing of juvenile offenders on recidivism, the effect of the minimum wage and unemployment insurance on employment, and the effect of preschooling on high school graduation.

Chapter 3 continues to study prediction of policy outcomes, addressing problems more challenging than those examined in Chapter 2. Again the problem is to predict the outcomes that would occur under a policy mandating some treatment. The fresh challenge is that no one in the observed study population received the treatment that would be mandated. The identical-response assumptions studied in Chapter 2 have no power to predict the outcomes of an entirely new treatment.

An approach that can make prediction possible is to make assumptions about how individuals respond to treatment. This idea has long been used by economists who seek to predict behavioral response to new policy. I describe and critique the economic practice of *revealed preference analysis,* which combines basic assumptions of rational choice behavior with more specific assumptions about the preferences that people hold. To illustrate, I discuss research that aims to learn how labor supply responds to income taxation and how college enrollment responds to federal financial aid policy.

Having explained the immense difficulty of predicting policy outcomes in Part I, I consider in Part II how decision making may reasonably cope with this difficulty. Chapter 4 examines policy choice by a *planner,* a real or idealized decision maker who acts on behalf of society. I use basic principles of decision theory to frame the problem of planning with partial knowledge. These principles do not give a complete guide to policy choice in an uncertain world. To the contrary, they make clear that there exists no uniquely correct way to cope with partial knowledge, only various reasonable ways. To illustrate, I discuss how police might choose to search for evidence of crime when they have partial knowledge of the deterrent effect of search. And I consider how a public health planner who has partial knowledge of disease transmission might choose a policy of vaccination against infectious disease.

Chapter 5 applies the framework for planning with partial knowledge to the problem of allocating a population to two treatments. I propose *diversified treatment choice* as a strategy to cope with uncertainty and reduce it over time. Financial diversification has long been a familiar recommendation for portfolio allocation, where an investor allocates wealth across a set of investments that have unknown returns. I argue that diversification may also be appealing when a society must treat a population of persons and does not know the best treatment.

The rationale for treatment diversification strengthens further when the task is to sequentially treat successive new cohorts of persons. We may now benefit from learning, with observation of the outcomes experienced by earlier cohorts informing treatment choice for later cohorts. I point out that diversification is advantageous for learning because it randomly assigns persons to treatments and thus generates randomized experiments. This leads me to introduce the idea of *adaptive diversification,* in which society updates its treatment allocation over time as information about treatment response accumulates. To illustrate, I consider provision of medical treatments in centralized health care systems and the drug approval process of the Food and Drug Administration.

Chapter 6 ties Parts I and II together. I discuss the institutional separation of policy analysis and decision making in modern societies. And I suggest that society view the relationship between policy analysis and decisions as a question of treatment response. Alternative approaches to policy analysis are treatments, and the quality of policy decisions is an outcome of concern to society.

I

POLICY ANALYSIS

1

⇒•◦•⇐

Policy Analysis with Incredible Certitude

To BEGIN, I distinguish the logic and the credibility of policy analysis (Section 1.1) and cite arguments made for certitude (Section 1.2). I then develop a typology of practices that contribute to incredible certitude. I call these practices *conventional certitudes* (Section 1.3), *dueling certitudes* (Section 1.4), *conflating science and advocacy* (Section 1.5), *wishful extrapolation* (Section 1.6), *illogical certitude* (Section 1.7), and *media overreach* (Section 1.8). In each case, I provide illustrations.

1.1. The Logic and Credibility of Policy Analysis

Policy analysis, like all empirical research, combines assumptions and data to draw conclusions about a population of interest. The logic of empirical inference is summarized by the relationship:

$$\text{assumptions} + \text{data} \rightarrow \text{conclusions}.$$

Data alone do not suffice to draw conclusions. Inference requires assumptions that relate the data to the population of interest. (One may ask what role theory plays in the logic of inference. Theory and assumptions are synonyms. I mainly use the latter term, reserving the former for broad systems of assumptions. Other synonyms for assumption are hypothesis, premise, and supposition.)

Holding fixed the available data, and presuming avoidance of errors in logic, stronger assumptions yield stronger conclusions. At the extreme, one may achieve certitude by posing sufficiently strong assumptions. The fundamental difficulty of empirical research is to decide what assumptions to maintain.

Given that strong conclusions are desirable, why not maintain strong assumptions? There is a tension between the strength of assumptions and their credibility. I have called this (Manski 2003, p. 1):

The Law of Decreasing Credibility: The credibility of inference decreases with the strength of the assumptions maintained.

This "law" implies that analysts face a dilemma as they decide what assumptions to maintain: Stronger assumptions yield conclusions that are more powerful but less credible.

I will use the word *credibility* throughout this book, but I will have to take it as a primitive concept that defies deep definition. The second edition of the *Oxford English Dictionary* (*OED*) defines *credibility* as "the quality of being credible." The *OED* defines *credible* as "capable of being believed; believable." It defines *believable* as "able to be believed; credible." And so we come full circle.

Whatever credibility may be, it is a subjective concept. Each person assesses credibility on his or her own terms. When researchers largely agree on the credibility of certain assumptions or conclusions, they may refer to this agreement as "scientific consensus." Persons sometimes push the envelope and refer to a scientific consensus as a "fact" or a "scientific truth." This is overreach. Consensus does not imply truth. Premature scientific consensus sometimes inhibits researchers from exploring fruitful ideas.

Disagreements occur often. Indeed, they may persist without resolution. Persistent disagreements are particularly common when assumptions are *nonrefutable*—that is, when alternative assumptions are consistent with the available data. As a matter of logic alone, disregarding credibility, an analyst can pose a nonrefutable assumption and adhere to it forever in the absence of disproof. Indeed, he can displace the burden of proof, stating "I will maintain this assumption until it is proved wrong." Analysts often do just this. An observer may question the credibility of a nonrefutable assumption, but not the logic of holding on to it.

To illustrate, American society has long debated the deterrent effect of the death penalty as a punishment for murder. Disagreement persists in part because empirical research based on available data has not been able to settle the question. With this background, persons find it tempting to pose their personal beliefs as a hypothesis, observe that this hypothesis cannot be rejected empirically, and conclude that society should act as if their personal belief is correct. Thus, a person who believes that there is no deterrent effect may state that, in the absence of credible evidence for deterrence, society should act as if there is no deterrence. Contrariwise, someone who believes that the death penalty does deter may state that, in the absence of credible evidence for no deterrence, society should act as if capital punishment does deter. I will discuss deterrence and the death penalty further in Chapter 2.

1.2. Incentives for Certitude

A researcher can illuminate the tension between the credibility and power of assumptions by posing alternative assumptions of varying credibility and determining the conclusions that follow in each case. In practice, policy analysis tends to sacrifice credibility in return for strong conclusions. Why so?

A proximate answer is that analysts respond to incentives. I have earlier put it this way (Manski 2007a, 7–8):

> The scientific community rewards those who produce strong novel findings. The public, impatient for solutions to its pressing concerns, rewards those who offer simple analyses leading to unequivocal policy recommendations. These incentives make it tempting for researchers to maintain assumptions far stronger than they can persuasively defend, in order to draw strong conclusions.
>
> The pressure to produce an answer, without qualifications, seems particularly intense in the environs of Washington, D.C. A perhaps apocryphal, but quite believable, story circulates about an economist's attempt to describe his uncertainty about a forecast to President Lyndon B. Johnson. The economist presented his forecast as a likely range of values for the quantity under discussion. Johnson is said to have replied, 'Ranges are for cattle. Give me a number.'

When a president as forceful as Johnson seeks a numerical prediction with no expression of uncertainty, it is understandable that his advisers feel compelled to comply.

Jerry Hausman, a longtime econometrics colleague, stated the incentive argument this way at a conference in 1988, when I presented in public my initial findings on policy analysis with credible assumptions: "You can't give the client a bound. The client needs a point." (A bound is synonymous with a range or an interval. A point is an exact prediction.)

Hausman's comment reflects a perception that I have found to be common among economic consultants. They contend that policy makers are either psychologically unwilling or cognitively unable to cope with uncertainty. Hence, they argue that pragmatism dictates provision of point predictions, even though these predictions may not be credible.

This psychological-cognitive argument for certitude begins from the reasonable premise that policy makers, like other humans, have limited willingness and ability to embrace the unknown. However, I think it too strong to draw the general conclusion that "the client needs a point." It may be that some persons think in purely deterministic terms. However, a considerable body of research measuring expectations shows that most make sensible probabilistic predictions when asked to do so; see Chapter 3 for further discussion and references. I see no reason to expect that policy makers are less capable than ordinary people.

Support for Certitude in Philosophy of Science

The view that analysts should offer point predictions is not confined to U.S. presidents and economic consultants. It has a long history in the philosophy of science.

Over fifty years ago, Milton Friedman expressed this perspective in an influential methodological essay. Friedman (1953) placed prediction as the central objective of science, writing (p. 5): "The ultimate goal of a positive science is the development of a 'theory' or 'hypothesis' that yields valid and meaningful (i.e. not truistic) predictions about phenomena not yet observed." He went on to say (p. 10):

> The choice among alternative hypotheses equally consistent with the available evidence must to some extent be arbitrary, though there is general agreement that relevant considerations are suggested by the criteria 'simplicity' and 'fruitfulness,' themselves notions that defy completely objective specification.

Thus, Friedman counseled scientists to choose one hypothesis (that is, make a strong assumption), even though this may require the use of "to some extent . . . arbitrary" criteria. He did not explain why scientists should choose a single hypothesis out of many. He did not entertain the idea that scientists might offer predictions under the range of plausible hypotheses that are consistent with the available evidence.

The idea that a scientist should choose one hypothesis among those consistent with the data is not peculiar to Friedman. Researchers wanting to justify adherence to a particular hypothesis sometime refer to *Ockham's Razor*, the medieval philosophical declaration that "plurality should not be posited without necessity." The *Encyclopaedia Britannica Online* (2010) gives the usual modern interpretation of this cryptic statement, remarking that "the principle gives precedence to simplicity; of two competing theories, the simplest explanation of an entity is to be preferred." The philosopher Richard Swinburne writes (1997, 1):

> I seek . . . to show that—other things being equal—the simplest hypothesis proposed as an explanation of phenomena is more likely to be the true one than is any other available hypothesis, that its predictions are more likely to be true than those of any other available hypothesis, and that it is an ultimate a priori epistemic principle that simplicity is evidence for truth.

The choice criterion offered here is as imprecise as the one given by Friedman. What do Britannica and Swinburne mean by "simplicity"?

However one may operationalize the various philosophical dicta for choosing a single hypothesis, the relevance of philosophical thinking to policy analysis is not evident. In policy analysis, knowledge is instrumental to the objective of making good decisions. When philosophers discuss the logical foundations and human construction of knowledge, they do so without posing this or another explicit objective. Does use of criteria such as "simplicity" to choose one hypothesis among those consistent with the data promote good policy making? This is the relevant question for policy analysis. As far as I am aware, philosophers have not addressed it.

1.3. Conventional Certitudes

John Kenneth Galbraith popularized the term *conventional wisdom*, writing (1958, chap. 2): "It will be convenient to have a name for the ideas which are esteemed at any time for their acceptability, and it should be a term that emphasizes this predictability. I shall refer to these ideas henceforth as the conventional wisdom." The entry in Wikipedia (2010) nicely put it this way:

> Conventional wisdom (CW) is a term used to describe ideas or explanations that are generally accepted as true by the public or by experts in a field. The term implies that the ideas or explanations, though widely held, are unexamined and, hence, may be reevaluated upon further examination or as events unfold. . . . Conventional wisdom is not necessarily true.

I shall similarly use the term *conventional certitude* to describe predictions that are generally accepted as true, but that are not necessarily true.

CBO Scoring of Pending Legislation

In the United States today, conventional certitude is exemplified by Congressional Budget Office (CBO) *scoring* of pending federal legislation. I will use CBO scoring as an extended case study.

The CBO was established in the Congressional Budget Act of 1974. Section 402 states (Committee on the Budget, U.S. House of Representatives, 2008, 39–40):

> The Director of the Congressional Budget Office shall, to the extent practicable, prepare for each bill or resolution of a public character reported by any committee of the House of Representatives or the Senate (except the Committee on Appropriations of each House), and submit to such committee—(1) an estimate of the costs which would be incurred in carrying out such bill or resolution in the fiscal year in which it is to become effective and in each of the 4 fiscal years following such fiscal year, together with the basis for each such estimate;

This language has been interpreted as mandating the CBO to provide point predictions (scores) of the budgetary impact of pending legislation. Whereas the 1974 legislation called for prediction five years into the future, the more recent practice has been to forecast ten years out. CBO scores are conveyed in letters that the director writes to leaders of Congress and chairs of congressional committees. They are not accompanied by measures of uncertainty, even though legislation often proposes complex changes to federal law, whose budgetary implications must be difficult to foresee.

Serious policy analysts recognize that scores for complex legislation are fragile numbers, derived from numerous untenable assumptions. Considering the closely related matter of scoring the effects of tax changes on federal revenues, Auerbach wrote (1996, 156): "in many instances, the uncertainty is so great that one honestly could report a number either twice or half the size of the estimate actually reported."

Credible scoring is particularly difficult to achieve when proposed legislation may significantly affect the behavior of individuals and firms, by changing the incentives they face to work, hire, make purchases, and so on. Academic economists, who have the luxury of studying subjects for years, have worked long and hard to learn how specific elements of public policy affect individual and firm behavior, but with only limited success. CBO analysts face the more difficult challenge of forecasting the effects of the many policy changes that may be embodied in complex legislation, and they must do so under extreme time pressure.

In light of the above, it is remarkable that CBO scores have achieved broad acceptance within American society. In our highly contentious political age, the scores of pending legislation have been eagerly awaited by both Democratic and Republican members of Congress. And media reports largely take them at face value.

Scoring the Patient Protection and Affordable Care Act of 2010

CBO scoring of the major health care legislation enacted in 2009–2010 illustrates well current practice. Throughout the legislative process, Congress and the media paid close attention to the scores of alternative bills considered by various congressional committees. A culminating event occurred on March 18, 2010, when the CBO, assisted by staff of the Joint Committee on Taxation (JCT), provided a preliminary score for the combined consequences of the Patient Protection and Affordable Care Act and the Reconciliation Act of 2010. CBO director Douglas Elmendorf wrote to House of Representatives Speaker Nancy Pelosi (Elmendorf 2010a, 2): "CBO and JCT estimate that enacting both pieces of legislation . . . would produce a net reduction of changes in federal deficits of $138 billion over the 2010–2019 period as a result of changes in direct spending and revenue."

Anyone seriously contemplating the many changes to federal law embodied in this legislation should recognize that the $138 billion prediction of deficit reduction can be no more than a very rough estimate. However, the twenty-five-page letter from Elmendorf to Pelosi expressed no uncertainty and did not document the methodology generating the prediction.

Media reports largely accepted the CBO scores as fact, the hallmark of conventional certitude. For example, a March 18, 2010, *New York Times* article documenting how CBO scoring was critical in shaping the legislation reported (Herszenhorn 2010): "A preliminary cost estimate of the final legislation, released by the Congressional Budget Office on Thursday, showed that the President got almost exactly what he wanted: a $940 billion price tag for the new insurance coverage provisions in the bill, and the reduction of future federal deficits of $138 billion over 10 years." The *Times* article did not question the validity of the $940 and $138 billion figures.

Interestingly, the certitude that CBO expressed when predicting budgetary impacts ten years into the future gave way to considerable uncertainty when considering longer horizons. In his letter to Pelosi, Director Elmendorf wrote (p. 3):

> Although CBO does not generally provide cost estimates beyond the 10-year budget projection period, certain Congressional rules require some information about the budgetary impact of legislation in subsequent decades. . . . Therefore, CBO has developed a rough outlook for the decade following the 2010–2019 period. . . . Our analysis indicates that H.R. 3590, as passed by the Senate, would reduce federal budget deficits over the ensuing decade relative to those projected under current law—with a total effect during that decade that is in a broad range between one-quarter percent and one-half percent of gross domestic product (GDP).

Further insight into the distinction that the CBO drew between the ten-year and longer horizons emerges from a March 19 letter that the director wrote to Congressman Paul Ryan (Elmendorf 2010b, 3):

> A detailed year-by-year projection, like those that CBO prepares for the 10-year budget window, would not be meaningful over a longer horizon because the uncertainties involved are simply too great. Among other factors, a wide range of changes could occur—in people's health, in the sources and extent of their insurance coverage, and in the de-

livery of medical care (such as advances in medical research, technological developments, and changes in physicians' practice patterns)—that are likely to be significant but are very difficult to predict, both under current law and under any proposal.

Thus, the CBO was quick to acknowledge uncertainty when asked to predict the budgetary impact of the health care legislation more than ten years out, phrasing its forecast as a "broad range" rather than as a point estimate.

Why did the CBO express uncertainty only when making predictions beyond the ten-year horizon? Longer-term predictions may be more uncertain than shorter-term ones, but it is not reasonable to set a discontinuity at ten years, with certitude expressed up to that point and uncertainty only beyond it. The potential behavioral changes cited by Elmendorf in his letter to Ryan, particularly changes in insurance coverage and in physicians' practice patterns, could occur soon after passage of the new legislation.

Having discussed scoring practices with various CBO personnel, I am confident that Director Elmendorf recognized the ten-year prediction sent to Speaker Pelosi was at most a rough estimate. However, he felt compelled to adhere to the established CBO practice of expressing certitude when providing ten-year predictions, which play a formal role in the congressional budget process.

A similar tension between unofficial recognition of uncertainty and official expression of certitude is evident in a U.S. Department of Health and Human Services (HHS) document (Foster 2010) that reports independent estimates of the budgetary implications of the health care legislation. The HHS document, like the CBO letter, provides point estimates with no accompanying measures of uncertainty. However, HHS verbally cautions (p. 19) that the estimates are uncertain:

> Due to the very substantial challenges inherent in modeling national health reform legislation, our estimates will vary from those of other experts and agencies. Differences in results from one estimating entity to another may tend to cause confusion among policy makers. These differences, however, provide a useful reminder that all such estimates are uncertain and that actual future impacts could differ significantly from the estimates of any given organization. Indeed, the future costs and coverage effects could lie outside of the range of estimates provided by the various estimators.

Credible Interval Scoring

Since its creation in 1974, the CBO has established and maintained an admirable reputation for impartiality. Perhaps it is best to leave well enough alone and have the CBO continue to express certitude when it scores pending legislation, even if the certitude is only conventional rather than credible.

I understand the temptation to leave well enough alone, but I think it unwise to try to do so. I would like to believe that Congress will make better decisions if the CBO provides it with credible predictions of budgetary impacts. Whether or not this is a reasonable expectation, I worry that someday sooner or later the existing social contract to take CBO scores at face value will break down. Conventional certitudes that lack foundation cannot last indefinitely. I think it better for the CBO to preemptively act to protect its reputation than to have some disgruntled group in Congress or the media declare that the emperor has no clothes.

It has been suggested that, when performing its official function of scoring legislation, the CBO is required to provide no more than a single point estimate. For example, in a 2005 article, CBO analyst Benjamin Page wrote (Page 2005, 437):

> Scoring has a specific meaning in the context of the federal budget process. Under the Congressional Budget Act of 1974, the Congressional Budget Office provides a cost estimate, or "score," for each piece of legislation that is reported by a Congressional committee. . . . By its nature, the cost estimate must be a single point estimate.

However, my reading of the Congressional Budget Act suggests that the CBO is not prohibited from presenting measures of uncertainty when performing its official function of scoring.

A document on the congressional budget describes the process for modifying the CBO scoring procedure. Committee on the Budget, U.S. House of Representatives (2008, 156) states:

> These budget scorekeeping guidelines are to be used by the House and Senate Budget Committees, the Congressional Budget Office, and the Office of Management and Budget (the "scorekeepers") in measuring compliance with the Congressional Budget Act of 1974 (CBA), as amended, and GRH 2 as amended. The purpose of the guidelines is to

ensure that the scorekeepers measure the effects of legislation on the deficit consistent with established scorekeeping conventions and with the specific requirements in those Acts regarding discretionary spending, direct spending, and receipts. These rules shall be reviewed annually by the scorekeepers and revised as necessary to adhere to the purpose. These rules shall not be changed unless all of the scorekeepers agree. New accounts or activities shall be classified only after consultation among the scorekeepers. Accounts and activities shall not be reclassified unless all of the scorekeepers agree.

This passage indicates that the CBO cannot unilaterally change its scoring procedure, but that change can occur if the various "scorekeepers" agree.

Presuming that the CBO can express uncertainty, how should it do so? There is no uniquely correct answer to this question, and alternatives may range from verbal descriptors to provision of probabilistic predictions. Aiming to balance simplicity and informativeness, I suggest provision of interval predictions of the budgetary impacts of legislation. Stripped to its essentials, computation of an interval prediction just requires that the CBO produce two scores for a bill, a low score and a high score, and report both. If the CBO must provide a point prediction for official purposes, it can continue to do so, choosing a point within the interval prediction.

Interval scoring is not an entirely new idea. A version of it was briefly entertained by Alan Auerbach in the article mentioned earlier. Auerbach (1996) wrote, "Presumably, forecasters could offer their own subjective confidence intervals for the estimates they produce, and this extra information ought to be helpful for policymakers." He went on to caution, "However, there is also the question of how well legislators without formal statistical training would grasp the notion of a confidence interval."

The CBO need not describe its interval predictions as confidence intervals in the formal sense of statistical theory, where they are used to summarize imprecise knowledge stemming from observations of small samples of populations. The main sources of uncertainty about budgetary impacts are not statistical in nature; that is, they are not problems of inference from a sample to a population. They are rather that analysts are not sure what assumptions are realistic when they make predictions. A CBO interval prediction would be more appropriately described as the result of a sensitivity analysis, describing the sensitivity of predictions to variation in maintained assumptions.

Can Congress Cope with Uncertainty?

I have received disparate reactions when I have suggested interval CBO scoring to other economists and policy analysts. Academics usually react positively, but persons who have worked within the federal government tend to be skeptical. Indeed, former CBO director Douglas Holtz-Eakin told me that he expected Congress would be highly displeased if the CBO were to provide it with interval scores.

The arguments that I have heard against interval scoring have been of two types. One is the psychological-cognitive argument discussed in Section 1.2. The other begins by observing that Congress is not an individual, but rather a collection of persons with differing beliefs and objectives who must jointly make policy choices in a political decision process. Thus, congressional decision making should be conceptualized as a game.

In a game, the usual economic presumption that more information yields better decisions need not apply. Players possessing more information may adopt strategies that yield better or worse outcomes. It depends on the structure of the game and the objectives of the players.

Viewing congressional policy choice as a game legitimately counters wishful thinking that a Congress receiving credible scores would necessarily make better decisions. However, game theory does not generically support the contention that current CBO practice should be preferred to credible scoring. Whether game theory can generate useful normative conclusions about scoring is an open question.

British Norms

Curiously, the antipathy toward measurement of government forecast uncertainty evident in Washington, D.C., is not as apparent in London, UK. Since 1996, the Bank of England has regularly published probabilistic inflation forecasts presented visually as a "fan chart" (Britton, Fisher, and Whitley 1998). The fan chart provides a succinct and informative measurement of forecast uncertainty.

More recently, it has become official government policy to require an Impact Assessment (IA) for legislation submitted to Parliament. The government specifically asks that a sensitivity analysis be performed, providing this guidance to agencies in its Impact Assessment Toolkit (Department for Business, Innovation and Skills 2011, 23): "In order to reflect the inherent uncertainty of costs and benefits estimates, you may need to provide a range for your costs and benefits estimates."

The norms for government forecasting in the United Kingdom thus differ from those in the United States. I do not have a clear sense why this is the case.

1.4. Dueling Certitudes

A rare commentator who rejected the CBO prediction that the health care legislation would reduce the budget deficit by $138 billion was Douglas Holtz-Eakin, its former director. He dismissed the CBO score and offered his own (Holtz-Eakin 2010): "In reality, if you strip out all the gimmicks and budgetary games and rework the calculus, a wholly different picture emerges: The health care reform legislation would raise, not lower, federal deficits, by $562 billion." The CBO and Holtz-Eakin scores differed hugely, by $700 billion. Yet they shared the common feature of certitude. Both were presented as exact, with no expression of uncertainty.

This provides an example of *dueling certitudes*. Holtz-Eakin did not assert that the CBO committed a logical error. He instead questioned the assumptions maintained by the CBO in performing its derivation, and he asserted that a very different result emerges under alternative assumptions that he preferred. Each score may make sense in its own terms, each combining available data with assumptions to draw logically valid conclusions. Yet the two scores are sharply contradictory.

Anyone familiar with the style of policy analysis regularly practiced within the Washington Beltway, and often well beyond it, will immediately recognize the phenomenon of dueling certitudes. To illustrate, I will draw on my experience a decade ago chairing a National Research Council committee on illegal drug policy (National Research Council 1999, 2001).

The RAND and IDA Reports on Illegal Drug Policy

During the mid-1990s, two studies of cocaine control policy played prominent roles in discussions of federal policy toward illegal drugs. One was performed by analysts at RAND (Rydell and Everingham 1994) and the other by analysts at the Institute for Defense Analyses (IDA) (Crane, Rivolo, and Comfort 1997). The two studies posed similar hypothetical objectives for cocaine-control policy, namely reduction in cocaine consumption in the United States by 1 percent. Both studies predicted the monetary cost of using certain policies to achieve this objective. However, RAND and IDA used different assumptions and data to reach dramatically different policy conclusions.

The authors of the RAND study specified a model of the supply and demand for cocaine that aimed to formally characterize the complex interaction of producers and users and the subtle process through which alternative cocaine-control policies may affect consumption and prices. They used this model to evaluate various demand-control and supply-control policies and reached this conclusion (p. xiii):

> The analytical goal is to make the discounted sum of cocaine reductions over 15 years equal to 1 percent of current annual consumption. The most cost-effective program is the one that achieves this goal for the least additional control-program expenditure in the first projection year. The additional spending required to achieve the specified consumption reduction is $783 million for source-country control, $366 million for interdiction, $246 million for domestic enforcement, or $34 million for treatment. . . . The least costly supply-control program (domestic enforcement) costs 7.3 times as much as treatment to achieve the same consumption reduction.

The authors of the IDA study examined the time-series association between source-zone interdiction activities and retail cocaine prices. They reached an entirely different policy conclusion (p. 3):

> A rough estimate of cost-effectiveness indicates that the cost of decreasing cocaine use by one percent through the use of source-zone interdiction efforts is on the order of a few tens of millions of dollars per year and not on the order of a billion dollars as reported in previous research [the RAND study]. The differences are primarily attributed to a failure in the earlier research to account for the major costs imposed on traf-

fickers by interdiction operations and overestimation of the costs of conducting interdiction operations.

Thus, the IDA study specifically rebutted a key finding of the RAND study.

When they appeared, the RAND and IDA studies drew attention to the ongoing struggle over federal funding of drug control activities. The RAND study was used to argue that funding should be shifted toward drug treatment programs and away from activities to reduce drug production or to interdict drug shipments. The IDA study, undertaken in part as a reanalysis of the RAND findings, was used to argue that interdiction activities should be funded at present levels or higher.

At a congressional hearing, Lee Brown, then director of the Office of National Drug Control Policy (ONDCP), used the RAND study to argue for drug treatment (Subcommittee on National Security, International Affairs, and Criminal Justice, 1996, p. 61):

> Let me now talk about what we know works in addressing the drug problem. There is compelling evidence that treatment is cost-effective and provides significant benefits to public safety. In June 1994, a RAND Corporation study concluded that drug treatment is the most cost-effective drug control intervention.

In a subsequent hearing specifically devoted to the IDA study, Subcommittee Chair William Zeliff used the study to argue for interdiction (Subcommittee on National Security, International Affairs, and Criminal Justice 1998, 1):

> We are holding these hearings today to review a study on drug policy, a study we believe to have significant findings, prepared by an independent group, the Institute for Defense Analysis, at the request of Secretary of Defense Perry in 1994. . . . The subcommittee has questioned for some time the administration's strong reliance on treatment as the key to winning our Nation's drug war, and furthermore this subcommittee has questioned the wisdom of drastically cutting to the bone interdiction programs in order to support major increases in hardcore drug addiction treatment programs. The basis for this change in strategy has been the administration's reliance on the 1994 RAND study.

The National Research Council Assessment

At the request of ONDCP, the National Research Council (NRC) Committee on Data and Research for Policy on Illegal Drugs assessed the RAND and IDA studies. This assessment was published as a committee report (National Research Council 1999).

After examining the assumptions, data, methods, and findings of the two studies, the NRC committee concluded that neither constitutes a persuasive basis for the formation of cocaine control policy. The committee summarized its assessment of the RAND study as follows (p. 28):

> The RAND study is best thought of as conceptual research offering a coherent way to think about the cocaine problem. The study documents a significant effort to identify and model important elements of the market for cocaine. It represents a serious attempt to formally characterize the complex interaction of producers and users and the subtle process through which alternative cocaine-control policies may affect consumption and prices. The study establishes an important point of departure for the development of richer models of the market for cocaine and for empirical research applying such models to evaluate alternative policies.
>
> However, the RAND study does not yield usable empirical findings on the relative cost-effectiveness of alternative policies in reducing cocaine consumption. The study makes many unsubstantiated assumptions about the processes through which cocaine is produced, distributed, and consumed. Plausible changes in these assumptions can change not only the quantitative findings reported, but also the main qualitative conclusions of the study. . . . Hence the study's findings do not constitute a persuasive basis for the formation of cocaine control policy.

It summarized its assessment of the IDA study this way (p. 43):

> The IDA study is best thought of as a descriptive time-series analysis of statistics relevant to analysis of the market for cocaine in the United States. The study makes a useful contribution by displaying a wealth of empirical time-series evidence on cocaine prices, purity, and use since 1980. Efforts to understand the operation of the market for cocaine must be cognizant of the empirical data. The IDA study presents many of those data and calls attention to some intriguing empirical associations among the various series.
>
> However, the IDA study does not yield useful empirical findings on the cost-effectiveness of interdiction policies to reduce cocaine consump-

tion. Major flaws in the assumptions, data, and methods of the study make it impossible to accept the IDA findings as a basis for the assessment of interdiction policies. For example, the conclusions drawn from the data rest on the assumption that all time-series deviations in cocaine price from an exponential decay path should be attributed to interdiction events, not to other forces acting on the market for cocaine. Numerous problems diminish the credibility of the cocaine price series developed in the study, and an absence of information prevents assessment of the procedure for selecting interdiction events.

Thus, the committee concluded that neither the RAND nor the IDA study provides a credible estimate of what it would cost to use alternative policies to reduce cocaine consumption in the United States.

When I think now about the RAND and IDA studies, I consider their many specific differences to be less salient than their shared lack of credibility. Each study may be coherent internally, but each rests on such a fragile foundation of weak data and unsubstantiated assumptions as to undermine its findings. To its great frustration, the NRC committee had to conclude that the nation should not draw even the most tentative policy lessons from either study. Neither yields usable findings.

What troubles me most about both studies is their injudicious efforts to draw strong policy conclusions. It is not necessarily problematic for researchers to try to make sense of weak data and to entertain unsubstantiated conjectures. However, the strength of the conclusions drawn in a study should be commensurate with the quality of the evidence. When researchers overreach, they not only give away their own credibility, but they diminish public trust in science more generally. The damage to public trust is particularly severe when researchers inappropriately draw strong conclusions about matters as contentious as drug policy.

1.5. Conflating Science and Advocacy

I earlier summarized the logic of inference in empirical research by the relationship "assumptions + data → conclusions." Holding fixed the available data, the scientific method supposes that the directionality of inference runs from left to right. One poses assumptions and derives conclusions. However, one can reverse the directionality, seeking assumptions that imply predetermined conclusions. The latter practice characterizes advocacy.

Policy analysts inevitably portray their deliberative processes as scientific. Yet some analysis may be advocacy wrapped in the rhetoric of science. Studies published by certain think tanks seem almost inevitably to reach strong liberal or conservative policy conclusions. The conclusions of some academic researchers are similarly predictable. Perhaps these analysts begin without preconceptions and are led by the logic of inference to draw strong conclusions. Or they may begin with conclusions they find congenial and work backward to support them.

In the late 1980s, when I visited Washington often as director of the Institute for Research on Poverty, a thoughtful senior congressional staffer named Scott Lilly told me that he found it prudent to view all policy analysis as advocacy. Lilly remarked that he preferred to read studies performed by think tanks with established reputations as advocates to ones performed by ostensibly neutral academic researchers. He said that he often felt able to learn from the think-tank studies, because he was aware of the biases of the authors. In contrast, he found it difficult to learn from academic research by authors who may have biases but attempt to conceal them.

Milton Friedman, whom I have previously quoted, had a seductive ability to conflate science and advocacy. I give one illustration here. See Krugman (2007) for a broader portrait of Friedman as scientist and advocate.

Friedman and Educational Vouchers

Proponents of educational vouchers for school attendance have argued that American school finance policy limits the options available to students and impedes the development of superior educational alternatives. Government operation of free public schools, they say, should be replaced by vouchers permitting students to choose any school meeting specified standards. The voucher idea has a long history. Tom Paine proposed a voucher plan in 1792, in *The Rights of Man*. The awakening of modern interest is usually credited to Friedman (1955, 1962). His writing on the subject is emblematic of analysis that conflates science and advocacy.

Friedman cited no empirical evidence relating school finance to educational outcomes. He posed a purely theoretical classical economic argument for vouchers, which began as follows (Friedman 1955):

> The role assigned to government in any particular field depends, of course, on the principles accepted for the organization of society in general. In what follows, I shall assume a society that takes freedom of the individual, or more realistically the family, as its ultimate objective, and seeks to further this objective by relying primarily on voluntary exchange among individuals for the organization of economic activity. In such a free private enterprise exchange economy, government's primary role is to preserve the rules of the game by enforcing contracts, preventing coercion, and keeping markets free. Beyond this, there are only three major grounds on which government intervention is to be justified. One is "natural monopoly" or similar market imperfection which makes effective competition (and therefore thoroughly voluntary exchange) impossible. A second is the existence of substantial "neighborhood effects," i.e., the action of one individual imposes significant costs on other individuals for which it is not feasible to make him compensate them or yields significant gains to them for which it is not feasible to make them compensate him—circumstances that again make voluntary exchange impossible. The third derives from an ambiguity in the ultimate objective rather than from the difficulty of achieving it by voluntary exchange, namely, paternalistic concern for children and other irresponsible individuals.

He went on to argue that the "three major grounds on which government intervention is to be justified" justify government supply of educational vouchers but not government operation of free public schools, which he referred to as "nationalization" of the education industry.

Repeatedly, Friedman entertained a ground for government operation of schools and then dismissed it. Here is an excerpt from his discussion of the neighborhood-effects argument:

> One argument from the "neighborhood effect" for nationalizing education is that it might otherwise be impossible to provide the common core of values deemed requisite for social stability. . . . This argument has considerable force. But it is by no means clear. . . . that it is valid. . . .
>
> Another special case of the argument that governmentally conducted schools are necessary to keep education a unifying force is that private schools would tend to exacerbate class distinctions. Given greater

freedom about where to send their children, parents of a kind would flock together and so prevent a healthy intermingling of children from decidedly different backgrounds. Again, whether or not this argument is valid in principle, it is not at all clear that the stated results would follow.

This passage is intriguing. Friedman cited no empirical evidence regarding neighborhood effects, nor did he call for research on the subject. Instead, he simply stated "it is by no means clear" and "it is not at all clear" that neighborhood effects warrant public schooling.

Rhetorically, Friedman placed the burden of proof on free public schooling, effectively asserting that vouchers are the preferred policy in the absence of evidence to the contrary. This is the rhetoric of advocacy, not science. An advocate for public schooling could just as well reverse the burden of proof, arguing that the existing educational system should be retained in the absence of evidence. The result would be dueling certitudes.

As I have discussed (Manski 1992), a scientific analysis would have to acknowledge that economic theory per se does not suffice to draw conclusions about the optimal design of educational systems. It would have to stress that the merits of alternative designs depend on the magnitudes and natures of the market imperfections and neighborhood effects that Friedman noted as possible justifications for government intervention. And it would have to observe that information about these matters was almost entirely lacking when Friedman wrote in the mid-1950s. Indeed, much of the needed information remains lacking today.

1.6. Wishful Extrapolation

The second edition of the *Oxford English Dictionary* defines *extrapolation* as "the drawing of a conclusion about some future or hypothetical situation based on observed tendencies." Extrapolation in this sense is essential to the use of data in policy analysis. Policy analysis is not just historical study of observed tendencies. A central objective is to inform policy choice by predicting the outcomes that would occur if past policies were to be continued or alternative ones were to be enacted.

While I am hesitant to second-guess the *OED*, I think it important to observe that its definition of extrapolation is incomplete. The logic of inference does not enable any conclusions about future or hypothetical situations to be drawn based on observed tendencies per se. Assumptions are essential. Thus, I will amend the *OED* definition and say that extrapolation is "the drawing of a conclusion about some future or hypothetical situation based on observed tendencies and maintained assumptions."

Given available data, the credibility of extrapolation depends on what assumptions are maintained. Researchers often use untenable assumptions to extrapolate. I will refer to this manifestation of incredible certitude as *wishful extrapolation*.

Perhaps the most common extrapolation practice is to assume that a future or hypothetical situation is identical to an observed one in some respect. Analysts regularly make such *invariance* assumptions, sometimes with good reason but often without basis. Certain invariance assumptions achieve the status of conventional certitudes, giving analysts license to pose them without fear that their validity will be questioned.

I first describe a prominent case of wishful extrapolation, paraphrasing the discussion of selective incapacitation in Manski (1995, 2007a). I then discuss extrapolation from randomized experiments, using the drug approval process of the Food and Drug Administration to illustrate.

Selective Incapacitation

In 1982, the RAND Corporation released a study of criminal behavior as reported to researchers in 1978 by a sample of prison and jail inmates in California, Michigan, and Texas (Chaiken and Chaiken 1982; Greenwood and Abrahamse 1982). Most respondents reported that they had committed five or fewer crimes per year in the period before their current arrest and conviction. A small group reported much higher rates of crime commission, in some cases more than one hundred per year.

The researchers found a strong within-sample empirical association between various personal characteristics (past convictions, drug use, and employment history) and the event that a sample member had been a high-rate offender. This finding suggested to part of the research team that *selective incapacitation* should be encouraged as a crime-fighting tool (Greenwood and Abrahamse 1982). Selective incapacitation calls for the sentencing of convicted criminals to be tied to predictions of their future criminality. Those with backgrounds that predict high rates of offenses would receive longer prison terms than those with other backgrounds.

The RAND study generated much controversy, especially when a prediction approach devised by Greenwood found its way into legislative proposals for selective incapacitation (see Blackmore and Welsh 1983 and Blumstein et al. 1986). Some of the controversy concerned the normative acceptability of selective incapacitation, but much of it concerned the credibility of extrapolation from the RAND findings.

The findings characterized the empirical association between background and reported crime commission within one cohort of inmates imprisoned in three states under the sentencing policies then in effect. Would this association continue to hold when applied to other cohorts of inmates in other states? Would it hold when applied to convicted criminals who are not imprisoned under existing sentencing policies? Would it hold if sentencing policy were to change? In particular, would it hold if selective incapacitation were to be implemented?

The RAND study did not address these questions. Greenwood's approach to prediction of criminality simply assumed that the empirical association between background and reported crime commission would remain approximately the same when extrapolated to other times, places, and sentencing policies. As I see it, this invariance assumption was wishful extrapolation.

Extrapolation from Randomized Experiments: The FDA Drug Approval Process

The great appeal of randomized experiments is that they often deliver credible certitude about the outcomes of policies within a population under study. Standard experimental protocol calls for specification of a study population from which random samples of persons are drawn to form treatment groups. All members of a treatment group are assigned the same treatment.

Assume that treatment response is *individualistic*—that is, each person's outcome depends only on his own treatment, not on those received by other members of the study population. Then the distribution of outcomes realized by a treatment group is the same (up to random sampling error) as would occur if this treatment were assigned to all members of the population. Thus, when the assumption of individualistic treatment response is credible, a randomized experiment enables one to draw credible sharp conclusions about the outcomes that would occur if a policy were to be applied to the entire study population.

A common problem of policy analysis is to extrapolate experimental findings to a policy under consideration. To accomplish this, analysts regularly assume that the distribution of outcomes that would occur under the policy of interest would be the same as the distribution of outcomes realized by a specific experimental treatment group. This invariance assumption sometimes is reasonable, but often it is wishful extrapolation.

There are many reasons why policies of interest may differ from those studied in experiments, making the invariance assumption suspect. I will discuss three here. The use of randomized experiments to inform policy choice has been particularly important in medicine. I will use the drug approval process of the Food and Drug Administration (FDA) to illustrate.

The Study Population and the Population of Interest

The study populations of randomized experiments often differ from the population of policy interest. Participation in experiments cannot be mandated in democracies. Hence, study populations consist of persons who volunteer to participate. Experiments reveal the distribution of treatment response among these volunteers, not within the population to whom a policy would be applied.

Consider the randomized clinical trials (RCTs) performed by pharmaceutical firms to obtain FDA approval to market new drugs. The volunteer participants in these trials may not be representative of the relevant patient population. The volunteers are persons who respond to the financial and medical incentives offered by pharmaceutical firms. Financial incentives may be payment to participate in a trial or receipt of free treatments. The medical incentive is that participation in a trial gives a person a chance of receiving new drugs that are not otherwise available.

The study population materially differs from the relevant patient population if treatment response in the group who volunteer for a trial differs from treatment response among those who do not volunteer.

When the FDA uses trial data to make drug approval decisions, it im-
plicitly assumes that treatment response in the patient population is
similar to that observed in the trial. The accuracy of this invariance assumption may not be known.

The Experimental Treatments and the Treatments of Interest

The treatments assigned in experiments often differ from those that
would be assigned in actual policies. Consider again the RCTs performed
for drug approval. These trials are normally double-blinded, with neither the patient nor his physician knowing the assigned treatment.
Hence, a trial reveals the distribution of response in a setting where
patients and physicians are uncertain what drug a patient receives. It
does not reveal what response would be in a real clinical setting where
patients and physicians would have this information and be able to react
to it.

Another source of difference between the treatments assigned in
experiments and those that would be assigned in actual policies occurs
when evaluating vaccines for prevention of infectious disease. The
assumption of individualistic treatment response traditionally made in
analysis of experiments does not hold when considering vaccines, which
may not only protect the person vaccinated but also lower the rate at
which unvaccinated persons become infected. A vaccine is *internally*
effective if it generates an immune response that prevents a vaccinated
person from becoming ill or infectious. It is *externally* effective to the
extent that it prevents transmission of disease to members of the population who are unvaccinated or unsuccessfully vaccinated.

A standard RCT enables evaluation of internal effectiveness, but
does not reveal the external effect of applying different vaccination rates
to the population. If the experimental group is small relative to the size
of the population, the vaccination rate is essentially zero. If a trial vaccinates a non-negligible fraction of the population, the findings only
reveal the external effectiveness of the chosen vaccination rate. They
do not reveal what the population illness rate would be with other vaccination rates.

The Outcomes Measured in Experiments and the Outcomes of Interest

A serious measurement problem occurs when studies have short durations. We often want to learn long-term outcomes of treatments, but

short studies reveal only immediate outcomes. Credible extrapolation from such *surrogate outcomes* to the long-term outcomes of interest can be highly challenging.

Again, the RCTs for drug approval provide a good illustration. The most lengthy, called phase 3 trials, typically run for only two to three years. When trials are not long enough to observe the health outcomes of real interest, the practice is to measure surrogate outcomes and base drug approval decisions on their values. For example, treatments for heart disease may be evaluated using data on patient cholesterol levels and blood pressure rather than data on heart attacks and life span. In such cases, which occur regularly, the trials used in drug approval only reveal the distribution of surrogate outcomes in the study population, not the distribution of outcomes of real health interest.

Health researchers have called attention to the difficulty of extrapolating from surrogate outcomes to health outcomes of interest. Fleming and Demets (1996), who review the prevalent use of surrogate outcomes in phase 3 trials evaluating drug treatments for heart disease, cancer, HIV/AIDS, osteoporosis, and other diseases, write (p. 605): "Surrogate end points are rarely, if ever, adequate substitutes for the definitive clinical outcome in phase 3 trials."

The FDA and Conventional Certitude

The FDA drug approval process is more transparent than CBO scoring of legislation, the governmental prediction process considered earlier in this chapter. The FDA process clearly values credibility, as shown in its insistence on evidence from RCTs and on trial sizes adequate to bound the statistical uncertainty of findings. However, the FDA makes considerable use of conventional certitudes when it attempts to extrapolate from RCT data to predict the effectiveness and safety of new drugs in practice.

The approval process essentially assumes that treatment response in the relevant patient population will be similar to response in the study population. It assumes that response in clinical practice will be similar to response with double-blinded treatment assignment. And it assumes that effectiveness measured by outcomes of interest will be similar to effectiveness measured by surrogate outcomes. These assumptions often are unsubstantiated and sometimes may not be true, but they have become enshrined by long use.

Campbell and the Primacy of Internal Validity

The FDA is not alone in abstracting from the problem of extrapolation in analysis of randomized experiments. This is also characteristic of the social-science research paradigm emerging from the influential work of Donald Campbell.

Campbell distinguished between the internal and external validity of a study of treatment response. A study is said to have *internal validity* if its findings for the study population are credible. It has *external validity* if an invariance assumption permits credible extrapolation. Campbell discussed both forms of validity, but he argued that studies should be judged primarily by their internal validity and only secondarily by their external validity (Campbell and Stanley 1963; Campbell 1984).

This perspective has been used to argue for the universal primacy of experimental research over observational studies, whatever the study population may be. The reason given is that properly executed randomized experiments have high internal validity. The same perspective has been used to argue that the best observational studies are those that most closely approximate randomized experiments. The statistician Paul Rosenbaum put it this way (Rosenbaum 1999, 263):

> In a well-conducted laboratory experiment one of the rarest of things happens: The effects caused by treatments are seen with clarity. Observational studies of the effects of treatments on human populations lack this level of control but the goal is the same. Broad theories are examined in narrow, focused, controlled circumstances.

Rosenbaum, like Campbell, downplayed the importance of having the study population be similar to the population of policy interest, writing (p. 259): "Studies of samples that are representative of populations may be quite useful in describing those populations, but may be ill-suited to inferences about treatment effects."

Agreeing with Campbell and Rosenbaum, many researchers prefer achieving credible certitude about an easy-to-study population to achieving credible partial knowledge about the population of policy interest. A common practice has been to report the "effect of treatment on the treated," where "the treated" are the members of a study population who actually received a specified treatment (see, for example, Bloom 1984, Angrist 1990, Gueron and Pauly 1991, and Dubin and

Rivers 1993). Attempting to cope with the problem of noncompliance in randomized experiments, Imbens and Angrist (1994) and Angrist, Imbens, and Rubin (1996) recommend that treatment effects be reported for the subpopulation of "compliers," these being persons who would comply with their designated experimental treatments whatever they might be.

These ideas have noticeably affected governmental decision making. A prominent case is the FDA drug approval process, which only considers experimental evidence when making decisions on drug approval. Another is the Education Sciences Reform Act of 2002 (Public Law 107-279), which provides funds for improvement of federal educational research. The act defines a scientifically valid educational evaluation as one that "employs experimental designs using random assignment, when feasible, and other research methodologies that allow for the strongest possible causal inferences when random assignment is not feasible." The term "strongest possible causal inference" has been interpreted to mean the highest possible internal validity. No weight is given to external validity.

Unfortunately, analyses of experimental data have tended to be silent on the problem of extrapolating from the experiments performed to policies of interest. For example, the influential analyses of welfare reform experiments reported in Gueron and Pauly (1991) only described the mean outcomes experienced by the various treatment groups. One can use the reported experimental findings to predict policy outcomes only if one is willing to take the findings at face value, accepting their internal validity and not questioning their external validity. One is at a loss to interpret the findings otherwise.

From the perspective of policy choice, it makes no sense to value one type of validity above the other. What matters is the informativeness of a study for policy making, which depends jointly on internal and external validity. Hence, research should strive to measure both types of validity.

1.7. Illogical Certitude

I have thus far discussed research practices that are not credible but are logical. Errors in logic also contribute to incredible certitude. Errors may be mundane mistakes in computation or algebra, or, more seriously, they may be non sequiturs. Non sequiturs generate pseudo conclusions and hence yield misplaced certitude.

A common non sequitur occurs when a researcher performs a statistical test of some null hypothesis, finds that the hypothesis is not rejected, and interprets non-rejection as proof that the hypothesis is correct. Texts on statistics routinely caution that non-rejection does not prove a null hypothesis is correct. It only indicates the absence of strong evidence that the hypothesis is incorrect. Nevertheless, researchers sometimes confuse statistical non-rejection with proof.

A more exotic non sequitur has persisted in research on the heritability of human traits, which has often been wrongly interpreted to have implications for social policy. I will use this as an extended case study.

Heritability

Heritability has been a persistent topic of study and controversy since the latter third of the nineteenth century. The beginning of formal research is usually attributed to the British scientist Francis Galton, who appears to have been the first to attempt to distinguish the roles of "nature" and "nurture." About one hundred years after Galton started his studies, controversy about the heritability of IQ flared in the 1960s and 1970s. This subject has been particularly heated because some social scientists have sought to connect heritability of IQ with social policy, asserting that policy can do little to ameliorate inequality of achievement if IQ is largely heritable.

Considering the state of thinking in the late 1970s, Goldberger (1979) began a cogent critique of research on heritability this way (p. 327):

> When we look across a national population, we see large differences in intelligence as measured by IQ tests. To what extent are those differences the result of differences in genetic make-up, and to what extent are they the result of differences in life experience? What proportion of the variance in IQ test scores is attributable to genetic variance, and what proportion to environmental variance? This question has fascinated mankind—or at least the Anglo-American academic subspecies—for several generations. The fascination, I suppose, arises from the notion that the answer has some relevance to social policy: if IQ variance is largely genetic, then it is natural, just and immutable; but if

IQ variance is largely environmental, then it is unnatural, unjust and easily eradicated.

Goldberger concluded that heritability, whether it be of IQ or other traits, is irrelevant to social policy. I will explain why here. However, I first need to explain what the heritability statistic measures and how it has been interpreted.

Lay people often use the word "heritability" in the loose sense of the second edition of the *Oxford English Dictionary*, which defines it as "the quality of being heritable, or capable of being inherited." However, formal research on heritability uses the word in a specific technical way. Stripped to its essentials, heritability research seeks to perform an analysis of variance, a descriptive statistical procedure I will now explain.

Consider a population of persons. Heritability researchers pose an equation of the form

$$\text{outcome} = \text{genetic factors} + \text{environmental factors}$$

or, more succinctly, $y = g + e$. Here, y is a personal outcome (or phenotype), g symbolizes genetic factors, and e symbolizes environmental factors. It is commonly assumed that g and e are uncorrelated across the population. Then the ratio of the population variance of g to the variance of y is called the heritability of y. Researchers say that heritability gives the fraction of the variation in the outcome "explained by" or "due to" genetic factors.

The equation studied in heritability research poses an extraordinarily simple idealization of the complex process by which modern scientists believe that a person's genome and environment actually produce outcomes. The variables g and e respectively summarize the entire genome and the spectrum of environmental factors that may combine to determine outcomes. The equation supposes that g and e contribute additively to outcomes, rather than interact with one another. The assumption that g and e are uncorrelated is at odds with the reasonable conjecture that persons who inherit relatively strong genetic endowments tend to grow up in families with more favorable environments for child development.

The simplicity of the equation studied in heritability research presumably stems from the fact that this body of research began long before the genome was known to exist, never mind measured, and also well before population surveys reporting individual-specific data on environmental factors became available. In this historical context, g and e could not be observable measures of a person's genome and environment. They were metaphors, symbolic representations of hypothesized latent forces. The somewhat mystifying technical intricacies of heritability research—its reliance on outcome data for biological relatives, usually twins or siblings, and on various strong statistical assumptions—derived from the desire of researchers to make heritability estimable despite the fact that g and e were metaphorical.

What Does "More Important" Mean?

Suppose that a researcher obtains data on the outcomes experienced by twins or other relatives, makes enough assumptions, and reports an estimate of the heritability of the outcome. What does this number reveal that may be of interest?

Researchers often say that heritability measures the relative "importance" of genetic and environmental factors. A prominent example is *The Bell Curve*, where Herrnstein and Murray (1994, 135) proclaimed: "Cognitive ability is more important than parental SES [socioeconomic status] in determining poverty." Goldberger and Manski (1995) critique the analysis that underlies this and similar assertions.

The *Bell Curve* differed from traditional heritability research in some ways. In particular, Herrnstein and Murray observed their g and e, using statistically standardized measures of cognitive ability (g) and parental SES (e) obtained in a population survey. However, they shared the objective of assessing the relative importance of genetic and environmental factors in explaining the observed variation of population outcomes such as poverty. When they or other authors state that genetic differences are a "more important" source of outcome variation than differences in common environment, they apparently mean this in the tautological sense that the procedure used to decompose the observed variance in behavior attributes more of this variance to variation in the genetic factor g than to variation in a common (that is, family-specific) component of the environmental factor e.

Heritability and Social Policy

What has made research on heritability particularly controversial has been the inclination of researchers such as Herrnstein and Murray to interpret the magnitude of heritability estimates as indicators of the potential responsiveness of personal achievement to social policy. In particular, large estimates of heritability have been interpreted as implying small potential policy effectiveness.

A notable example was given by Goldberger (1979). Discussing a *Times* of London report of research relating genetics to earnings and drawing implications for social policy, he wrote (p. 337):

> For a more recent source we turn to the front page of The Times (13 May 1977), where under the heading "Twins show heredity link with earnings" the social policy correspondent Neville Hodgkinson reported:
>
>> A study of more than two thousand pairs of twins indicates that genetic factors play a huge role in determining an individual's earning capacity. . . . According to some British researchers, the study provides the best evidence to date in the protracted debate over the respective contributions of genetics and environment to an individual's fate. . . . The findings are significant for matters of social policy because of the implication that attempts to make society more equal by breaking "cycles of disadvantage" . . . are likely to have much less effect than has commonly been supposed.
>
> Professor Hans Eysenck was so moved by the twin study that he immediately announced to Hodgkinson that it "really tells the [Royal] Commission [on the Distribution of Income and Wealth] that they might as well pack up" (*The Times*, 13 May 1977).

Commenting on Eysenck, Goldberger continued (p. 337):

> (A powerful intellect was at work. In the same vein, if it were shown that a large proportion of the variance in eyesight were due to genetic causes, then the Royal Commission on the Distribution of Eyeglasses might as well pack up. And if it were shown that most of the variation in rainfall is due to natural causes, then the Royal Commission on the Distribution of Umbrellas could pack up too.)

This parenthetical passage, displaying Goldberger's characteristic combination of utter seriousness and devastating wit, shows the absurdity of considering heritability estimates to be policy relevant. Goldberger concluded (p. 346): "On this assessment, heritability estimates serve no worthwhile purpose."

It is important to understand that Goldberger's conclusion did not rest on the metaphorical nature of *g* and *e* in heritability research. It was based, more fundamentally, on the fact that variance decompositions do not yield findings of policy relevance.

To place heritability research on the best imaginable footing, suppose that g and e are not metaphors but rather are observable summary statistics for a person's genome and environment. Suppose that the equation $y = g + e$ is a physical law showing how the genome and environment combine to determine outcomes. Also suppose that g and e are uncorrelated in the population, as is typically assumed in heritability research. Then a researcher who observes the population may directly compute the heritability of y, without the need for special data on twins or obscure assumptions.

At one extreme, suppose that the population is composed entirely of clones who face diverse environments. Then the variance of g is zero, implying that heritability is zero. At the other extreme, suppose that the population is composed of genetically diverse persons who share the same environment. Then the variance of e is zero, implying that heritability is one.

What does this have to do with policy analysis? Nothing. Policy analysis asks what would happen to outcomes if an intervention, such as distribution of eyeglasses, were to change persons' environments in some manner. Heritability is uninformative about this.

While Goldberger's eyeglasses example got to the heart of the logical problem with heritability research in a particularly succinct and effective way, he was not alone in grasping the irrelevance of heritability to policy. Writing contemporaneously, the statistician Oscar Kempthorne (1978, 1) summarized his view of the matter this way:

> The conclusion is that the heredity-IQ controversy has been a "tale full of sound and fury, signifying nothing." To suppose that one can establish effects of an intervention process when it does not occur in the data is plainly ludicrous.

Given that it was widely recognized more than thirty years ago that heritability research is irrelevant to policy, I find it both remarkable and disheartening that some have continued to assert its relevance subsequently. For example, Herrnstein and Murray (p. 109) did so in *The Bell Curve*, referring to "the limits that heritability puts on the ability to manipulate intelligence." Research on the heritability of all sorts of outcomes continues to appear regularly today. Recent studies tend not to explicitly refer to policy, but neither do they provide any other articulate interpretation of the heritability statistics they report. The work goes on, but I do not know why.

Gene Measurement

For over a hundred years, research relating genetics to human outcomes was crippled by two problems, one conceptual and the other technological. The conceptual problem was the focus of research attention on estimating heritability, producing claims of "importance" that served no worthwhile purpose. The technological problem was the absence of means to measure genes. The latter problem may have contributed to the former by stimulating researchers to invent the metaphorical g in the absence of gene measurements.

The conceptual problem has been understood since the 1970s, and the technological one has been overcome in the past decade. Progress in gene measurement has increasingly enabled collection of data on the expression of specific genes in large samples of individuals. It is becoming routine to ask the respondents to major household surveys to provide saliva from which DNA may be extracted.

Gene measurement replaces the metaphorical g of heritability research and the indicators of *The Bell Curve* with direct observation of pieces of the genome that may be used in all of the ways that researchers ordinarily use data on personal attributes. It transforms research relating human genetics to personal outcomes from a mystical exercise into ordinary science.

For example, Caspi et al. (2003) used longitudinal data from a representative birth cohort to study prediction of depression conditional on the expression of a specific gene and aspects of a person's environment. The authors found predictive power in interactions of the gene with stressful life events, rather than in the gene per se. The use of specific measured genes to predict personal outcomes is entirely out of the scope of heritability research, where g is a latent construct rather than an observed attribute. Moreover, heritability research traditionally assumes that gene-environment interactions such as those found by Caspi et al. do not exist. The equation $y = g + e$ that typically forms the starting point for analysis of heritability assumes that g and e contribute additively to outcomes. See Manski (2011c) for further discussion.

1.8. Media Overreach

Elected officials, civil servants, and the public rarely learn of policy analysis from the original sources. The writing in journal articles and research reports is usually too technical and jargon-laden for nonprofessionals to decipher. Broad audiences may learn of new findings from newspapers, magazines, and electronic media. The journalists and editors who decide what analysis warrants coverage and how to report it therefore have considerable power to influence societal perspectives.

Some media coverage of policy analysis is serious and informative, but overreach is all too common. When journalists and editors decide that research is newsworthy, they seem to rarely err on the side of overly cautious reporting. The prevailing view seems to be that certitude sells.

"The Case for $320,000 Kindergarten Teachers"

A conspicuous instance of media overreach appeared on the front page of the *New York Times* on July 28, 2010, in an article with the above title. There the *Times* economics columnist David Leonhardt reported on research investigating how students' kindergarten experiences affect their income as adults. Leonhardt began his article with the question "How much do your kindergarten teacher and classmates affect the rest of your life?" He then called attention to new work by a group of six economists that attempts to answer the question, at least with regard to adult income.

Characterizing the study's findings as "fairly explosive," Leonhardt focused most attention on the impact of good teaching. Referring by name to Raj Chetty, one of the authors, he wrote,

> Mr. Chetty and his colleagues . . . estimate that a standout kindergarten teacher is worth about $320,000 a year. That's the present value of the additional money that a full class of students can expect to earn over their careers.

Leonhardt concluded by making a policy recommendation, stating,

> Obviously, great kindergarten teachers are not going to start making $320,000 anytime soon. Still, school administrators can do more than

they're doing. They can pay their best teachers more . . . and give them the support they deserve. . . . Given today's budget pressures, finding the money for any new programs will be difficult. But that's all the more reason to focus our scarce resources on investments whose benefits won't simply fade away.

I have called Leonhardt's article media overreach. My reason was hinted at by Leonhardt when he wrote that the new study was "not yet peer-reviewed." In fact, the study did not even exist as a publicly available working paper when Leonhardt wrote his article. All that existed for public distribution was a set of slides for a July 2010 conference presentation made by the authors at the National Bureau of Economic Research (http://obs.rc.fas.harvard.edu/chetty/STAR_slides.pdf). A bullet point on the final page of the slides estimates the value of good kindergarten teaching to be $320,000. The slides do not provide sufficient information about the study's data and assumptions to enable an observer to assess the credibility of this estimate.

The study has subsequently been published (Chetty et al. 2011), so evaluation of its data and assumptions has become possible. However, when Leonhardt wrote his piece, the community of researchers in the economics of education had not yet had the opportunity to read or react to the new study, never mind to review it for publication. Nevertheless, Leonhardt touted the findings as definitive and used them to recommend policy. Surely this is incredible certitude. I think it highly premature for a major national newspaper to report at all on new research at such an early stage, and bizarre to place the report on the front page.

Peer Review and Credible Reporting

The 2010 *New York Times* article on kindergarten teaching is a striking case of reporting on research prior to peer review, but it is not unique. For example, the 1977 *Times* of London article on heritability cited in Section 1.7 reported the findings of an unpublished draft research paper.

Premature media reporting on research would lessen to some degree if the media would refrain from covering research that has not yet been vetted within the scientific community through an established peer-review process. However, journalists should not trust peer review per se to certify the logic or credibility of research. Anyone with experience submitting or reviewing articles for publication becomes aware that peer review is an imperfect human enterprise. Weak studies may be accepted for publication and strong studies rejected, even when peer reviewers do their best to evaluate research objectively. The trustworthiness of peer review is diminished further when reviewers use the process to push their own advocacy agendas, accepting studies whose conclusions they favor.

It is unquestionably difficult for journalists and editors, who cannot possibly be sufficiently expert to evaluate personally all policy analysis, to decide what studies to report and how to frame their coverage. Yet there are straightforward actions that they can take to mitigate media overreach. First and perhaps foremost, they can scrutinize research reports to assess whether and how the authors express uncertainty about their findings. They should be deeply skeptical of studies that assert certitude. When authors express uncertainty, journalists should pay close attention to what they say.

Second, journalists should not rely fully on what authors say about their own work. They should seek perspectives from relevant reputable researchers who are not closely associated with the authors. Careful journalists already do this, but the practice should become standard.

2

---◆◆◆---

Predicting Policy Outcomes

IN AN ideal world, persons who are not expert in research methodology would be able to trust the conclusions of policy analysis. They would be able to believe predictions of policy outcomes without concern about the process used to produce them.

Unfortunately, the practices described in Chapter 1 indicate that consumers of policy analysis cannot safely trust the experts. Civil servants, journalists, and concerned citizens need to understand prediction methods well enough to be able to assess reported findings. They need to comprehend conceptually, if not in technical detail, how predictions depend on maintained assumptions and available data.

With this in mind, Chapters 2 and 3 describe various conventional approaches that use strong assumptions to obtain strong conclusions. I additionally describe approaches that I have developed, which use weaker assumptions to obtain interval predictions. The two chapters study different prediction problems. This one mainly concerns a relatively simple yet subtle problem that arises in many applied settings and has drawn extraordinary research attention. Phrased abstractly, there are two feasible treatments, labeled A and B. The available data come from a study population where some persons received treatment A and some received B. The problem is to predict the outcomes that would occur under a policy mandating that everyone receive the same treatment. Section 2.1 gives an initial illustration, after which I begin to address the problem methodically in Section 2.2.

2.1. Deterrence and the Death Penalty

Researchers have long used data on homicide rates and sanctions to examine the deterrent effect of capital punishment. The subject became a concern beyond the academic community in the 1970s when the solicitor general of the United States (Bork et al. 1974) argued to the Supreme Court that a study by Isaac Ehrlich provided credible findings on the deterrent effect of capital punishment. Ehrlich (1975) used annual data on murders and sanctions in the United States to estimate a "murder supply" function specifying the murder rate that would occur as a function of sanction levels, including the risk of capital punishment faced by a convicted murderer. He concluded (p. 398):

> In fact, the empirical analysis suggests that on the average the tradeoff between the execution of an offender and the lives of potential victims it might have saved was of the order of 1 for 8 for the period 1933–1967 in the United States.

This finding, and its citation before the Supreme Court as evidence in support of the death penalty, generated considerable controversy. A panel of the National Research Council was established to investigate in depth the problem of inference on deterrence (Blumstein, Cohen, and Nagin 1978). In all, the NRC report presents an exceptionally clear-headed portrayal of some of the difficulties inherent in empirical study of deterrence.

The fundamental difficulty is that the outcomes of counterfactual policies are unobservable. Data alone cannot reveal what the homicide rate in a state with (or without) a death penalty would have been had the state not adopted (or adopted) a death penalty statute. Thus, data must be combined with assumptions to enable inference on counterfactual outcomes. The NRC panel observed that democratic societies ordinarily do not perform experiments that randomly assign persons to alternative sanctions policies. Hence, research on deterrence generally analyzes data from observational studies. The panel concluded that it is hard to find credible assumptions that, when combined with available data, reveal the deterrent effect of sanctions. The panel concluded (p. 62): "The current evidence on the deterrent effect of capital punishment is inadequate for drawing any substantive conclusion."

A large body of work has subsequently addressed deterrence and the death penalty, yet the literature has still failed to achieve consensus on even the most basic matters. The National Research Council recently convened a new Committee on Deterrence and the Death Penalty to assess the research undertaken since the Ehrlich study. This committee examined the numerous studies undertaken over the past thirty years but ultimately reiterated the conclusion of the earlier NRC report, stating (Committee on Deterrence and the Death Penalty 2012): "The committee concludes that research to date on the effect of capital punishment on homicide is not informative about whether capital punishment decreases, increases, or has no effect on homicide rates."

Estimates Using Data on Homicide Rates across States and Years

Much of the research literature has sought to infer the deterrent effect of the death penalty from data on homicide rates across states and years. However, the available data may be used in various ways, yielding different estimates.

To illustrate some of the possibilities in a simple setting, Manski and Pepper (2012) examined data from the critical 1970s period when the Supreme Court decided the constitutionality of the death penalty. The 1972 Supreme Court case *Furman v. Georgia* resulted in a multiyear moratorium on the application of the death penalty, while the 1976 case *Gregg v. Georgia* ruled that the death penalty could be applied subject to certain criteria. We examined the effect of death penalty statutes on homicide rates in two years: 1975, the last full year of the moratorium, and 1977, the first full year after the moratorium was lifted. In 1975 the death penalty was illegal throughout the country, and in 1977 thirty-two states had legal death penalty statutes. For each state and each year, we observe the homicide rate and whether the death penalty is legal.

Table 2.1 displays the homicide rate per 100,000 residents in 1975 and 1977 in the states that did and did not legalize the death penalty after the *Gregg* decision. We call the former the "treated" states and the latter the "untreated" ones. We regard the District of Columbia as equivalent to a state. When computing averages across states, we weight each state by its population. The thirty-two states with legal death penalty statutes in 1977 contained 70 percent of the total population.

Table 2.1   Homicide rates per 100,000 residents by year and treatment
              status in 1977

		Group	
Year	Untreated	Treated	Total
1975	8.0	10.3	9.6
1977	6.9	9.7	8.8
Total	7.5	10.0	9.2

The data in the table may be used to compute three simple estimates of the effect of death penalty statutes on homicide. A "before and
after" analysis compares homicide rates in the treated states in 1975
and 1977. The 1975 homicide rate in these states, when none had the
death penalty, was 10.3 per 100,000. The 1977 rate, when all had the
death penalty, was 9.7. The before-and-after estimate is the difference
between the 1977 and 1975 homicide rates; that is, -0.6 ($9.7 - 10.3$). This
is interpretable as the average effect of the death penalty on homicide in
the treated states if one assumes that nothing germane to homicide
occurred in these states between 1975 and 1977 except for legalization
of capital punishment. See Section 2.4 for further discussion of before-
and-after studies.

Alternatively, one might compare the 1977 homicide rates in the
treated and untreated states. The 1977 rate in the treated states, which
had the death penalty, was 9.7. The 1977 rate in the untreated states,
which did not have the death penalty, was 6.9. The estimate is the difference between these homicide rates; that is, 2.8 ($9.7 - 6.9$). This is interpretable as the nationwide average effect of the death penalty on
homicide in 1977 if one assumes that persons living in the treated and
untreated states have the same propensity to commit murder in the absence of the death penalty and respond similarly to enactment of the
death penalty. With this assumption, the observed homicide rate in the
treated states reveals what the rate would have been in the untreated
states if they had enacted the death penalty, and vice versa. See Section
2.5 for further discussion of this type of assumption, which is maintained in analysis of randomized experiments.

Yet a third way to use the data is to compare the temporal changes
in homicide rates in the treated and untreated states. Between 1975

and 1977, the homicide rate in the treated states fell from 10.3 to 9.7. In the same period, the rate in the untreated states fell from 8.0 to 6.9. The so-called *difference-in-difference* (DID) estimate is the difference between these temporal changes; that is, 0.5 [(9.7 − 10.3) − (6.9 − 8.0)]. This is interpretable as the nationwide effect of the death penalty on homicide if one assumes considerable homogeneity across states, specifically that all states experience a common time trend in homicide and that enactment of the death penalty has the same effect in all states. See Section 2.4 for further discussion of DID estimates and explanation of the assumptions that motivate them.

These three estimates yield different empirical findings regarding the effect of the death penalty on homicide. The before-and-after estimate implies that enactment of a death penalty statute reduces the homicide rate by 0.6 per 100,000. The other two estimates imply that having the death penalty raises the homicide rate by 2.8 or 0.5 per 100,000. The idea that capital punishment may increase the homicide rate is contrary to the traditional view of punishment as a deterrent. However, some researchers have argued that the death penalty shows a lack of concern for life that brutalizes society into greater acceptance of commission of murder. Thus, the old debate between those who believe the death penalty does or does not have a deterrent effect has been expanded to include a third possibility, that the death penalty has a *brutalization* effect.

Which estimate is correct? Given certain assumptions, each appropriately measures the effect of the death penalty on homicide. However, the assumptions that justify this interpretation differ across estimates. One may be correct, or none of them.

2.2. Analysis of Treatment Response

To begin our more formal analysis, I need to introduce some basic concepts. Borrowing a term from medicine, I will refer to prediction of the outcomes of alternative policies as *analysis of treatment response.*

One contemplates a policy that has been or may be applied to the members of a population, sometimes called *treatment units.* For example, a sentence decreed for a convicted offender is a treatment, the offender being the treatment unit. Similarly, an income tax levied by a government is a treatment. In this case, the treatment unit may be an individual, a married couple, a corporation, or another legal entity subject to income tax.

The outcome that a treatment unit would experience under a conjectured treatment is his *treatment response*. A simplifying assumption made regularly in analysis of treatment response is that response is *individualistic*. This means that the outcome of a person or other treatment unit may vary only with his own treatment, not with those of other members of the population. When this assumption does not hold, treatment response is said to have *social interactions*.

The credibility of assuming that response is individualistic varies with the context. One may think it plausible that medical treatment of diabetes affects only the person treated. However, one may not think it plausible that response to vaccination against infectious disease is individualistic. An important rationale for vaccination is to prevent the spread of disease. Vaccinating you may protect not only you but me as well.

Policy analysis uses data on a study population to predict policy outcomes in a population of interest. A *study population* is a group that has been subjected to a policy. A *population of interest* is simply a group whose outcomes one would like to predict.

A researcher observes outcomes experienced by members of the study population after a policy is implemented. He then combines these data with assumptions to predict the outcomes that would occur if a specified policy were to be implemented in the population of interest.

Statistical Inference and Identification

Statistical inference uses data on a sample of members of the study population to predict outcomes in the entire study population, under the policy actually implemented there. *Identification* analysis studies several forms of extrapolation from the study population. One may want to predict the outcomes of policies that were not implemented in the study population. One may want to predict different outcomes than those observed in the study population. Or one may want to predict the outcomes that would occur if the policy implemented in the study population were to be implemented in another population of interest.

To illustrate the distinction between statistical inference and identification, recall our discussion of the FDA drug approval process (Section 1.6). A sample of persons volunteer to participate in a clinical trial and are randomly assigned to treatments. A pharmaceutical firm wanting approval for a new drug uses the observed outcomes to test the hypothesis that the new drug works as well as a placebo against the alternative that it works better. This hypothesis test performs statistical inference, using the sample data to draw conclusions about the effectiveness of the drug in a study population of potential volunteers. The three forms of extrapolation discussed earlier—from a study population to an actual patient population, from blinded to unblinded treatment, and from surrogate outcomes to outcomes of interest—pose identification problems.

Statistical inference contributes to the difficulty of predicting policy outcomes, but increasing sample size improves the precision of predictions. In contrast, increasing sample size does not diminish identification problems. These usually are the dominant difficulties in prediction. I will focus on identification throughout the book. I will particularly emphasize the basic identification problem that stems from the unobservability of counterfactual outcomes.

To illustrate, consider judicial sentencing of convicted offenders. A policy maker choosing a sentencing policy would like to compare the recidivism that offenders would experience under alternative sentencing rules. One may be able to observe the recidivism of convicted offenders in a study population following the sentences that they actually receive. However, one cannot observe the recidivism that these offenders would have experienced had they received different sentences.

The unobservability of counterfactual outcomes is a matter of logic. It is not a practical problem resolvable by new data collection or by better measurement methods. It is a fundamental problem of empirical inference that can be addressed only by making assumptions that relate observed and counterfactual outcomes.

2.3. Predicting Outcomes under Policies That Mandate a Treatment

Most of this chapter discusses a relatively simple problem in analysis of treatment response, which has attracted much research attention. Suppose that each member of a study population may receive one of two treatments, say *A* or *B*. A status quo policy is in place, assigning some persons to treatment *A* and the remainder to *B*. One observes the treatments and outcomes realized by the study population—that is, the treatments they actually received and the outcomes they experienced. One assumes that treatment response is individualistic. One wants to predict the outcomes that would occur in the study population, or a new population with the same composition, if everyone were to receive the same treatment.

Sentencing and Recidivism

To illustrate the prediction problem, I will use the Manski and Nagin (1998) analysis of sentencing and recidivism of juvenile offenders in the state of Utah. Under the status quo policy, judges had the discretion to order various sentences. They gave some offenders sentences with no confinement (treatment *A*) and sentenced others to residential confinement (treatment *B*). Two alternatives to the status quo would be to replace judicial discretion with a mandate that all offenders be confined or a mandate that no offenders be confined. The problem is to predict recidivism under these alternative policies.

Background

Ample data are available on the outcomes experienced by juvenile offenders given the sentences that they actually receive. However, researchers have long debated the counterfactual outcomes that offenders would experience if they were to receive other sentences. There has been particular disagreement about the relative merits of confinement in residential treatment facilities and diversion to nonresidential treatment.

Confinement has been favored by the "medical model" of deviance, which views deviance as symptomatic of an underlying pathology that requires treatment. In this view, the juvenile justice system should determine the needs of the child and direct the treatment resources of the state to ameliorating those needs. Confinement is thought beneficial because it enables treatment.

Non-confinement has been favored by criminologists who are skeptical of the ability of the justice system to deliver effective treatment. This skepticism stems in part from the "labeling" view of deviance. According to this view, a constellation of negative consequences may flow from official processing of a juvenile as deviant, even with a therapeutic intent. Confinement in a residential facility may make it more likely that the person thinks of himself as deviant, may exclude him from the normal routines of life, and may place him into closer affinity with deviant others who may reinforce negative feelings the person has about himself. Given these concerns, labeling theorists have promoted the "secondary deviance" hypothesis, which holds that confinement is more likely to lead to recidivism than is nonresidential treatment.

To adjudicate between the competing predictions of the medical model and the secondary deviance hypothesis, it would be useful to perform experiments that randomly assign some offenders to confinement and others to nonresidential treatment. However, experimentation with criminal justice policy is difficult to implement. Hence, empirical research on sentencing and recidivism has relied on observational studies. Analysts have combined available data on sentencing outcomes with the strong but suspect assumption that judges randomly sentence offenders conditional on characteristics that are observable to researchers.

Our Analysis

Manski and Nagin (1998) implemented a cautious mode of "layered" analysis that begins with no assumptions about how judges sentence offenders and then moves from weak, highly credible assumptions to stronger, less credible ones. Exploiting the rich event-history data on juvenile offenders collected by the state of Utah, we presented several sets of findings and showed how conclusions about sentencing policy vary depending on the assumptions made.

We first reported interval predictions (or bounds) obtained without making any assumptions at all about the manner in which judges choose sentences. We assumed only that treatment response is individualistic. We then presented bounds obtained under two alternative models of judicial decision making. The *outcome optimization* model assumes judges make sentencing decisions that minimize the chance of recidivism. The *skimming* model assumes that judges classify offenders as "higher risk" or "lower risk," sentencing only the former to residential confinement. Each model expresses an easily understood hypothesis about judicial decision making. Finally, we brought to bear further

assumptions in the form of *exclusion restrictions*, which posit that specified subpopulations of offenders respond to sentencing similarly but
face different sentencing selection rules.

The empirical findings turned out to depend critically on the assumptions imposed. With nothing assumed about sentencing rules or
response, only weak conclusions could be drawn about the recidivism
implications of the two sentencing options. With assumptions made
about judicial decision making, the results were far more informative.
If one believes that Utah judges choose sentences in an effort to minimize recidivism, the empirical results point to the conclusion that residential confinement exacerbates criminality on average. If one believes
that judges behave in accord with the skimming model, the results suggest the opposite conclusion, namely that residential confinement has
an ameliorative effect on average. Imposition of an exclusion restriction strengthened each of these opposing conclusions.

Analysis Assuming Individualistic Treatment Response

I describe here the very simple analysis assuming only that treatment
response is individualistic. If treatment response is individualistic, the
recidivism that occurs for offenders sentenced to confinement under
the status quo policy would continue to occur under a new policy mandating confinement. The change in policy leaves their treatments un-
changed, and the treatments received by others do not affect their outcomes. Thus, the assumption of individualistic response reduces our
lack of knowledge to prediction of the recidivism of offenders who were
not confined under the status quo policy. If these persons were confined, it may be that none of them would commit another offense or
that they all would commit new offenses.

For simplicity, I measure recidivism as a binary (yes/no) event.
Thus, an offender is classified as a recidivist if he commits at least one
offense after sentencing and as a non-recidivist if he commits no offenses. Then the objective is to predict the recidivism rate when confinement is mandatory. This will be called R_{MB}, where R denotes recidivism
rate and MB denotes mandatory (M) assignment to treatment B. Similarly, R_{MA} is the recidivism rate when non-confinement is mandatory.

We can observe outcomes under the status quo policy. In particular, we observe the realized recidivism rate for offenders actually confined (say R_B), the realized recidivism rate for offenders actually not

confined (R_A), the fraction of offenders actually confined (F_B), and the fraction of offenders actually not confined (F_A). The fractions F_A and F_B sum to one.

The data and the assumption of individualistic response imply bounds on the recidivism rates R_{MB} and R_{MA} that would emerge under policies mandating one treatment or the other. I will focus on the former, as the derivation for the latter is analogous. The smallest possible value of R_{MB} would occur if no offender who was unconfined in the status quo would recidivate if he were confined. Then the recidivism rate would be the rate R_B for those actually confined times the fraction F_B of such persons in the population. The largest possible value would occur if all offenders unconfined in the status quo would recidivate if they were confined. Then R_{MB} would equal its lower bound plus the fraction F_A of such persons.

To summarize, the data and the assumption of individualistic response imply that the smallest possible value of R_{MB} is $R_B \times F_B$ and the largest possible value is $R_B \times F_B + F_A$. In succinct notation, the bound is

$$R_B \times F_B \leq R_{MB} \leq R_B \times F_B + F_A.$$

An analogous bound holds for the policy of mandatory non-confinement. Repetition of the derivation with B replacing A and vice versa shows that the bound on recidivism in this case is

$$R_A \times F_A \leq R_{MA} \leq R_A \times F_A + F_B.$$

These bounds show that treatment response is *partially* identified. The data and the assumption of individualistic response do not yield certitude about R_{MB} or R_{MA}, but they do yield bounds. To achieve certitude requires stronger assumptions that deliver *point* identification. That is, further assumptions are needed to narrow the bounds to points.

Numerical Findings

Numerically, the Utah data reveal that 11 percent of the convicted offenders were sentenced to confinement and that 77 percent of these persons recidivated; thus, $F_B = 0.11$ and $R_B = 0.77$. The remaining 89 percent were sentenced to non-confinement, and 59 percent of these persons recidivated; thus, $F_A = 0.89$ and $R_A = 0.59$. Hence, the lower bound on R_{MB} is 0.08 and the upper bound is 0.97. The bound has width 0.89 because 0.89 of all offenders were not confined under the status quo policy. We do not know what the recidivism of these persons would be under the policy of mandatory confinement.

The lower bound on R_{MA} is 0.53 and the upper bound is 0.64. The width 0.11 is the fraction of offenders who were confined under the status quo policy. Thus, the data reveal much more about recidivism with mandatory non-confinement than with mandatory confinement.

Choosing a Policy

To preview a type of decision problem that we will study in Part II of the book, suppose that the Utah legislature contemplates replacement of the status quo policy with mandatory confinement or non-confinement. Suppose there is consensus that the objective should be to minimize recidivism. Suppose legislators think it credible that treatment response is individualistic, but they do not think other assumptions to be plausible.

In this setting, legislators can predict that recidivism with mandatory confinement would lie in the range 0.08 to 0.97, whereas recidivism with mandatory non-confinement would lie in the range 0.53 to 0.64. They can compare these bounds with the known value of recidivism under the status quo policy. This is

$$R_S = R_A \times F_A + R_B \times F_B,$$

where S denotes the status quo policy. Numerically, R_S equals 0.61 using the Utah data. Thus, the policies mandating a specified treatment may yield lower or higher recidivism than the status quo. The legislature's problem is to choose a policy in this environment of ambiguity.

Observe that the recidivism rate under the status quo policy lies within the bounds on recidivism under both policies that eliminate judicial discretion. This is not happenstance. Inspection of the formulae for the bounds on R_{MB} and R_{MA} shows that R_S necessarily lies within both bounds, whatever values the data may take.

This algebraic finding has a simple explanation. Not observing counterfactual recidivism outcomes, one cannot refute the hypothesis that treatment does not affect recidivism. Under this hypothesis, R_S, R_{MB}, and R_{MA} all have the same value.

This is an important negative result. It shows that data on the outcomes of a status quo policy combined only with the assumption of individualistic response cannot determine whether a policy mandating a particular treatment performs better or worse than the status quo policy. Stronger assumptions are needed to rank the policies.

2.4. Identical Treatment Units

Analysts usually report point predictions of policy outcomes, not bounds. Beginning here and continuing throughout the chapter, I will describe various assumptions used to make point predictions and explain how they yield certitude.

Perhaps the most elementary idea is to assume that different treatment units respond to treatment identically. That is, if different units were to receive the same treatment, they would experience the same outcome. Assuming that treatment units are identical does not mean that they are identical in every respect, just that they respond to treatment in the same way.

Suppose that one wants to predict the outcomes of a policy in which all treatment units in a population of interest would receive treatment *B*. Consider such a unit and suppose one can find an identical unit in the study population that actually received treatment *B*. Then one can conclude that, if the former unit were to receive *B*, it would experience the outcome realized by the latter unit.

Controlled experiments in the natural sciences use this reasoning. The researcher prepares two specimens, intending them to be identical in every treatment-relevant respect. He applies treatment *B* to one specimen and observes the outcome. Assuming that the specimens respond to treatment identically, the observed outcome of the treated specimen is the outcome that the untreated one would experience if it were to receive treatment *B*.

When studying humans, analysts cannot prepare identical specimens. Persons inevitably are heterogeneous. Even so-called identical twins are only genetically identical, not identical in the environments that they face. Whether the context be educational or medical or criminal, persons may vary in their response to treatment. The same heterogeneity may occur when the treatment units are localities rather than persons. No two cities or states are identical. Nevertheless, analysts sometimes attempt to mimic the reasoning of controlled experiments.

They match units that appear similar and assume that these units respond identically to treatment.

Before-and-After Studies

A common practice is to compare outcomes in a single treatment unit at two points in time, before and after an event occurs. The unit's environment prior to occurrence of the event is treatment A, and its environment following the event is B. A *before-and-after study* assumes that, except for the occurrence of the event, the unit is identical at the earlier and later points in time.

This reasoning underlies the first estimate of the deterrent effect of the death penalty presented in Section 2.1. Recall that the estimate compared homicide rates in the treated states in 1975, when they did not have the death penalty, and 1977, when they did. Assuming that the treated states were identical treatment units in 1975 and 1977, the homicide rate observed in 1975 reveals what the rate would have been in 1977 in the absence of the death penalty. The homicide rate observed in 1977 reveals what the rate would have been in 1975 with the death penalty.

Another example is the IDA report on illegal-drug policy (Crane, Rivolo, and Comfort 1997) discussed in Section 1.4. The centerpiece of the IDA analysis was its juxtaposition of the time series of cocaine prices against the onset of eight major drug interdiction events initiated by the federal government. The data showed that a long-run downward trend in cocaine prices was interrupted by an abrupt and lasting change in 1989 and by a number of short-lived upward "excursions" that appeared from time to time. The IDA authors attributed these interruptions to the eight interdiction events, stating (pp. 1–2), "the sudden change in the price decay rate and each of the short-term excursions are shown to follow the initiation of major interdiction activities, primarily in the source zone nations, and are thus to be causally connected." Thus, IDA performed eight before-and-after studies. It assumed that, in all relevant respects except for the drug interdiction events, the market for cocaine operated identically in the periods before and after the interdiction events occurred.

The NRC committee reviewing the IDA study did not find this assumption credible. Recall that the committee wrote (National Research Council 1999, 43):

Major flaws in the assumptions, data, and methods of the study make it impossible to accept the IDA findings as a basis for the assessment of interdiction policies. For example, the conclusions drawn from the data rest on the assumption that all time-series deviations in cocaine price from an exponential decay path should be attributed to interdiction events, not to other forces acting on the market for cocaine.

Difference-in-Difference Studies

A variation on the idea of identical treatment units is assumed in the many empirical studies that report difference-in-difference estimates of treatment effects. These studies permit outcomes to vary across treatment units but assume that different units are identical in two respects: they experience a common time trend in outcomes and they respond identically to treatment.

Recall the third estimate of the deterrent effect of the death penalty presented in Section 2.1, which compared the temporal changes in homicide rates in the treated and untreated states between 1975 and 1977. This estimate can be motivated by the assumption that the homicide rate varies across states, years, and death penalty status as follows:

homicide rate with death penalty = state effect + year effect +
death-penalty effect

homicide rate without death penalty = state effect + year effect.

These equations permit states to have different homicide rates, but the additive year effect assumes a common time trend, and the additive death-penalty effect assumes identical response of the homicide rate to the death penalty in all states and years. Some manipulation of these equations (see Manski and Pepper 2012) yields the difference-in-difference estimate of the death-penalty effect, namely:

death-penalty effect = 1975–1977 change in observed homicide rate in
treated states – 1975–1977 change in observed homicide rate in
untreated states.

Employment in Fast-Food Restaurants and the Minimum Wage

A well-known application of this type of reasoning was performed by David Card and Alan Krueger (Card and Krueger 1994, 1995). Economists have long sought to evaluate the effect of the minimum wage on employment. Attempting to shed new light on this question, Card and Krueger compared the change in employment in fast-food restaurants in New Jersey and in eastern Pennsylvania that occurred between March 1992 and November 1992. In March 1992, both states had the same minimum wage of $4.25 per hour. In April 1992, the minimum wage in New Jersey was raised to $5.05, while that in Pennsylvania remained $4.25.

The authors reported the DID estimate

minimum-wage effect = March–November change in observed employment in New Jersey – March–November change in observed employment in Pennsylvania.

This estimate can be motivated by the assumption that employment varies across states, months, and minimum-wage level as follows:

employment with higher minimum wage = state effect + month effect + minimum-wage effect

employment with lower minimum wage = state effect + month effect.

These equations permit New Jersey and Pennsylvania to have different employment, but the month effect assumes a common time trend, and the minimum-wage effect assumes identical response of employment to the minimum wage across states and months.

The authors found that employment declined between March and November in Pennsylvania fast-food restaurants but not in New Jersey ones. They concluded (Card and Krueger 1994, 792):

> Contrary to the central prediction of the textbook model of the minimum wage, . . . we find no evidence that the rise in New Jersey's minimum wage reduced employment at fast-food restaurants in the state. . . . We find that the increase in the minimum wage increased employment.

Card and Krueger considered this and their findings in other studies destructive to the economic conventional wisdom about the minimum wage. They provocatively titled their 1995 book on the subject *Myth and Measurement: The New Economics of the Minimum Wage.*

To justify their assumption of identical treatment response, the authors wrote (p. 773):

> New Jersey is a relatively small state with an economy that is closely linked to nearby states. We believe that a control group of fast-food

stores in eastern Pennsylvania forms a natural basis for comparison with the experiences of restaurants in New Jersey.

However, some readers of their work were less certain whether treatment response was identical. For example, Kennan (1995) wrote in a cautious review article (p. 1958):

> Most people who have read an economics book (and many who have not) know what to expect in this experiment: employment should fall in New Jersey, and not in Pennsylvania, other things being equal. But what if other things are not equal? After all, we are comparing early spring with early winter, and a lot can happen in nine months. Then one must hope that changes in these other things affecting the fast food business in New Jersey are matched by similar changes in Pennsylvania. If so, the effect of the minimum wage increase will show up as the difference between the employment change in New Jersey and the change in Pennsylvania.

To Kennan, it was an open question whether comparison of employment changes in New Jersey and Pennsylvania approximates the conditions of a controlled experiment.

2.5. Identical Treatment Groups

While it rarely is credible to assume that individuals respond identically to treatment, it sometimes is credible to assume that treatment groups have identical response distributions. This idea underlies the appeal of randomized experiments. I explain here.

To begin, a *treatment group* is a collection of treatment units in a study population who receive the same treatment under the status quo policy. Thus, those who receive treatment *A* are one treatment group, and those who receive *B* are another group. In general, the members of a treatment group may be heterogeneous, each unit responding to treatment in his own way. The response distribution of a group describes this heterogeneity, giving the frequencies of different response patterns within the group. I will say that two treatment groups are identical if they have identical response distributions.

Illustration: Consider sentencing and recidivism. The treatment response of an offender is expressed by a pair of potential outcomes: (recidivism if not confined, recidivism if confined). Let the outcome equal one if an offender were to commit a new offense and zero if not. Then there are four possible response patterns: (0, 0), (0, 1), (1, 0), (1, 1). An offender has response pattern (0, 0) if he would not recidivate regardless of treatment, pattern (0, 1) if he would not recidivate under treatment *A* but would recidivate under treatment *B*, and so on.

The response distribution of a group of offenders is the frequency with which each of these response patterns occurs in the group. The groups of offenders who receive treatments *A* and *B* under the status quo policy have identical response distributions if each group has the same frequencies of the four patterns.

It is important to understand that treatment groups with identical response distributions need not have identical distributions of realized outcomes. The realized outcomes of the group receiving *A* are the outcomes they experience with this treatment. The realized outcomes of the group receiving *B* are the outcomes they experience with that treatment.

With this background, suppose that one wants to predict the outcomes of a policy mandating treatment *B*. Assume that treatment groups *A* and *B* are identical, in the sense of having identical response distributions. It follows that, if group *A* were to receive treatment *B*, their outcome distribution would be the same as the one actually realized by group *B*. Hence, the population outcome distribution under a policy mandating treatment *B* would be the same as the outcome distribution realized by group *B* under the status quo policy.

Assuming that treatment groups are identical is much weaker than assuming that treatment units are identical. It is reasonable to ask what one pays for weakening the assumption, from the perspective of predicting policy outcomes. The answer is straightforward. Assuming that units are identical enables one to predict the outcomes that particular persons would experience if they were to receive specified treatments. Assuming that groups are identical enables one to predict the population distribution of outcomes, but not the outcomes of particular persons.

The weaker assumption generally suffices. The usual objective of policy analysis is to predict population distributions of outcomes, not the outcomes of particular persons. For example, in our discussion of sentencing policy, I supposed that the legislature's objective is to minimize the rate of recidivism, not to minimize the recidivism of specific offenders.

Experiments with Random Assignment of Treatments

When should one believe that treatment groups are identical? In observational studies, where an analyst observes the outcomes of treatments selected in some decentralized manner, the assumption of identical groups is often suspect. For example, in a sentencing environment with judicial discretion, there may be no good reason to believe that the groups of offenders sentenced to confinement and non-confinement have the same distribution of treatment response.

Or consider the second estimate of the deterrent effect of the death penalty presented in Section 2.1, which compared the 1977 homicide rates in the treated and untreated states. This estimate is interpretable as the nationwide effect of the death penalty on homicide if one assumes that the residents of states which did and did not chose to enact the death penalty have the same propensities to commit murder. This may or may not be a reasonable assumption.

Yet the assumption of identical treatment groups has been a cornerstone of analysis of treatment response. The reason is that this assumption has high credibility when the status quo policy is a classical experiment with random assignment of treatments.

In a randomized experiment, two random samples of persons are drawn from a study population, with the members of one sample assigned to treatment A and the members of the other assigned to B. I will say that the experiment is "classical" if one assumes that treatment response is individualistic and if all subjects comply with their assigned treatments. These assumptions were made by the statistician R. A. Fisher in his highly influential early methodological studies of randomized experimentation (e.g., Fisher 1935), and they have been maintained regularly in applied research.

In a classical experiment, one random sample of persons receives treatment A and the other receives B. Random sampling implies that both treatment groups are likely to have distributions of treatment response that are similar to the population-wide response distribution, the degree of similarity increasing as the samples grow in size. Hence, it is credible to assume that the treatment groups stemming from a classical experiment with large samples of subjects are identical, or at least very similar.

The "Gold Standard"

While this is not the place for a full history, I think it important to describe some major developments in the use of randomized experiments in policy analysis. I will restrict attention to events in the United States.

Application of randomized clinical trials (RCTs) to learn about response to medical treatments took hold in the 1950s, particularly after an experiment with the new Salk polio vaccine credibly demonstrated the effectiveness of the vaccine. Performance of RCTs became a core requirement of the FDA drug approval process in 1962, with passage of amendments to the Food, Drug, and Cosmetics Act of 1938 (see Fisher and Moyé 1999). To signify their high regard for RCTs, medical researchers often refer to them as the "gold standard" for evidence on treatment response.

A notable early use of randomized experiments in policy analysis outside of medicine was the Perry Preschool Project, begun in the early 1960s. Intensive educational and social services were provided to a random sample of about sixty black children, ages three and four, living in a low-income neighborhood of Ypsilanti, Michigan. No special services were provided to a second random sample of such children drawn to serve as a control group. The treatment and control groups were subsequently followed into adulthood.

From the mid-1960s through the late 1970s, randomized experiments were used to evaluate such major proposed programs as the negative income tax and national health insurance. Various experiments of this period are described in Hausman and Wise (1985).

In the 1980s, randomized experiments came to dominate the evaluations of job training and welfare programs commissioned by the federal government and by major foundations. Dissatisfaction with observational studies of job training programs performed in the 1970s led the Department of Labor to commission an experimental evaluation of the Job Training Partnership Act in the mid-1980s. A set of experiments sponsored by the Ford Foundation and executed by the Manpower Demonstration Research Corporation influenced the federal government to choose experimental analysis as the preferred approach to evaluation of welfare reforms. The experiments of this period are described in Manski and Garfinkel (1992).

By the early 1990s, experimentation had become so much the orthodoxy that Jo Anne Barnhart, an assistant secretary of the U.S. Department of Health and Human Services in the first Bush administration, could write this about the evaluation of training programs for welfare recipients:

> In fact, nonexperimental research of training programs has shown such methods to be so unreliable, that Congress and the Administration have both insisted on experimental designs for the Job Training Partnership Act (JTPA) and the Job Opportunities and Basic Skills (JOBS) programs. (See U.S. General Accounting Office 1992, appendix 2)

Barnhart's reference to the unreliability of non-experimental research reflects the view of some social scientists that observational studies cannot provide a basis for credible inference on treatment response. Such authors as Bassi and Ashenfelter (1986) and LaLonde (1986) recommended that study of treatment response should focus exclusively on the design and analysis of randomized experiments. The sentiment that randomized experiments provide the best empirical basis for analysis of treatment response was evident in a National Research Council report on the evaluation of AIDS prevention programs, which declared (Coyle, Boruch, and Turner 1991, 125): "Well-executed randomized experiments require the fewest assumptions in estimating the effect of an intervention."

2.6. Randomized Experiments in Practice

When researchers say that randomized experiments constitute the "gold standard" for evidence on treatment response, they have in mind an ideal case where treatment response is individualistic, all subjects comply with their assigned treatments, and it is credible to extrapolate from the experiment to the question of policy interest. Experiments regularly deviate from this ideal in practice, often substantially so. I will discuss various reasons here.

Extrapolation

I called attention in Chapter 1 to several problems of extrapolation from RCTs that arise in the FDA drug-approval process. One of the problems discussed there, extrapolation from double-blinded treatment assignment to clinical practice, is specific to RCTs of drugs. However, the other problems occur regularly in randomized experiments that aim to inform policy analysis.

First, the study population in experiments often differs substantially from the population of policy interest. A cautionary example occurred in the experimental evaluation of the Job Training Partnership Act, cited favorably by Barnhart. The treatment units under the JTPA program were localities that offered training services to unemployed workers. The experimental design called for random selection of sites. However, evaluators did not have the power to compel localities to cooperate. Hotz (1992) describes how the JTPA evaluators originally sought to select sites randomly but, being unable to secure the agreement of the randomly drawn sites, were ultimately required to provide large financial incentives to nonrandomly selected localities in order to obtain their cooperation. One may reasonably question whether the distribution of treatment response in the cooperating sites was the same as in the nationwide population of localities with JTPA programs.

Second, randomized experiments often have short durations, forcing researchers to measure surrogate outcomes rather than outcomes of policy interest. We often want to learn long-term outcomes of treatments, but short studies reveal only immediate outcomes. For example, when considering preschool policy, society may want to know how policy affects adult outcomes including college enrollment, work experience, and criminality. However, studies of short duration can only measure outcomes that are observable when children are still young, such as test scores. Credible extrapolation from such surrogate outcomes to long-term outcomes of interest can be highly challenging.

A third matter is that it generally is impractical to evaluate experimentally all treatments of potential interest. This chapter, and a very large part of the literature on treatment response, simplifies real life considerably by supposing that the problem is to compare just two treatments, say A and B. However, the reality is that the treatments of interest may range from A to Z, and beyond. Samples of experimental subjects typically have limited size. Hence, experimental researchers focus on a small subset of the treatments that they would like to evaluate.

Compliance

A participant in an experiment is said to comply with treatment assignment if the treatment received is the same as the treatment assigned. In practice, noncompliance occurs as a consequence of choices made by the participants in experiments. Consider the RCTs performed for FDA drug approval. Subjects may be given a container of pills and instructed to take them on a prescribed schedule. However, some may not follow the instructions.

Manski (2007a, chap. 7) shows that, in the absence of assumptions on the compliance process, data from an experiment with partial compliance yield interval predictions of the outcomes of policies that mandate particular treatments. The derivation is similar to the one I gave in Section 2.3, in the context of sentencing and recidivism. Here I will discuss an experiment that aimed to inform labor market policy.

The Illinois Unemployment Insurance Experiment

The Illinois Unemployment Insurance Experiment was carried out in 1984–1985. Newly unemployed persons were randomly assigned to conventional unemployment insurance (UI) or to UI augmented by a wage subsidy paid to the employer if the unemployed person should find a full-time job within eleven weeks. An outcome of interest was whether an unemployed person found a full-time job within this time period.

Compliance was an issue, because participation in the subsidy-augmented version of UI could not be compelled. In practice, 32 percent of those assigned UI with the wage subsidy did not comply, choosing instead to receive conventional UI (see Dubin and Rivers 1993).

Suppose that the objective is to predict the outcomes that would occur if all unemployed persons were to receive the version of UI with the wage subsidy. The outcome of policy interest is binary, being success or failure in finding a new job within eleven weeks. The experiment revealed these outcomes for the 68 percent of subjects who complied with assignment to UI with the wage subsidy. It did not reveal the relevant outcomes for the 32 percent who chose not to comply. Hence, in the absence of assumptions about the nature of noncompliance, the experimental data yield an interval prediction of success in job search that has width 0.32.

Researchers analyzing experiments with partial compliance regularly report point rather than interval predictions of treatment response. To do so, some make assumptions about the nature of noncompliance. Others do not attempt to predict outcomes for a policy that mandates a particular treatment. I next discuss a leading case of each practice.

Random Compliance

Suppose that one knows which experimental subjects do and do not comply with their assigned treatments. This knowledge was available in the Illinois UI experiment, as each unemployed person had to enroll in one of the two versions of UI. It may not be available in RCTs where subjects self-administer their treatments and may not report their behavior accurately.

Researchers who observe compliance often assume that the groups who do and do not comply are identical, in the sense of having the same distribution of treatment response. Compliance is then said to be random. Given this assumption, the realized outcome distribution for subjects who comply with a particular treatment assignment is the same as the outcome distribution that would occur if the entire population were to receive this treatment.

The issue is the credibility of the assumption. Compliance is ordinarily a choice. There is often reason to think that persons who choose to comply and not comply have different distributions of treatment response.

In the Illinois UI experiment, it has been suggested that unemployed workers may have viewed the wage subsidy as stigmatizing. Hence, among subjects assigned the wage subsidy, those believing that they could find a job without the subsidy would choose to comply less often than those thinking their job prospects were dim. In RCTs, one might reasonably conjecture that subjects who experience lack of improvement in their medical condition choose to comply with assigned treatments less often than those who experience improvement.

Intention-to-Treat

Researchers sometimes do not attempt to predict outcomes for a policy that mandates a particular treatment. Instead, they specify study objectives that make noncompliance logically impossible.

Consider the common situation where A is a status quo treatment available to anyone in the population, while B is an innovation available only to experimental subjects assigned this treatment. Rather than predict the outcomes of a policy that mandates treatment B, researchers sometimes seek to predict the outcomes of a policy offering persons the option to choose B. They then interpret randomized assignment to treatment B as giving a subject an offer of B rather than mandating this treatment. This makes noncompliance logically impossible. The term *intention-to-treat* is used to describe an offer of a treatment.

Viewing treatment group B as receiving an offer rather than a mandate does not solve the original prediction problem but rather dismisses it by redefining the study objective. The original objective was to learn the outcomes that would occur if everyone were to actually receive treatment B. The redefined objective is to learn the outcomes that would occur if everyone were to receive an offer of this treatment, which they may either accept or reject.

To illustrate, consider again the Illinois UI experiment. Woodbury and Spiegelman (1987) described the experiment as randomly assigning unemployed persons to conventional UI or to an offer of UI with a wage subsidy, allowing the unemployed person to choose between conventional UI and the wage-subsidy-augmented UI. Hence, they were unconcerned with compliance and analyzed the experimental data in the classical manner. This contrasts with the Dubin and Rivers (1993) study mentioned above, which paid considerable attention to noncompliance.

The findings reported by Woodbury and Spiegelman differ from those by reported by Dubin and Rivers. In part, this is because the authors had different objectives. Woodbury and Spiegelman wanted to predict the outcomes that would occur if unemployed persons were permitted to choose between conventional UI and a program with a wage subsidy. Dubin and Rivers wanted to predict the outcomes that would occur if conventional UI were replaced by a program with a wage subsidy.

The Mixing Problem

Noncompliance may occur when an experiment offers a treatment, but the policy of interest would mandate this treatment. Conversely, the *mixing problem* arises when a randomized experiment mandates a treatment but the policy of interest would permit treatment units to choose between treatments.

I defined and studied the mixing problem in Manski (1997a). To illustrate, I considered the problem of predicting the outcomes of preschool policies. I will use this illustration to explain the nature of the problem.

Extrapolation from the Perry Preschool Project

Randomized experiments with preschool interventions have sought to learn the outcomes that occur when members of treatment and control groups respectively enroll and do not enroll in a new program. The usual objective has been to perform a classical experiment, with complete compliance to assigned treatments. If this succeeds, observation of the treatment and control groups reveals the outcomes that would occur if the program were mandated or unavailable.

Consider a policy that would offer a new program to parents but not mandate that they enroll their children. The experiment only partially reveals outcomes under this policy. Outcomes would depend on program participation and on the joint distribution of response to the two treatments, quantities that the experiment does not reveal. My study of the mixing problem showed what the experiment does reveal.

To give a numerical illustration, I took the subjects in the Perry Preschool Project to be the study population and interpreted the project as a classical randomized experiment. In this experiment, the high school graduation rate of the treatment group was 0.67 and that of the control group was 0.49. This evidence reveals what graduation rates would occur if the preschool treatment were respectively mandated or unavailable. However, the evidence does not reveal what graduation rate would occur if parents were offered the opportunity to enroll their children in preschool but not required to do so.

One might think that the graduation rate with an offer of preschool would necessarily fall between 0.49 and 0.67, the exact rate depending on program participation. This conclusion is correct if preschool can never make a child worse off than non-enrollment. It is also correct if parents would randomly decide whether to enroll their children in preschool. Suppose, however, that one finds neither assumption credible. My analysis showed that, if one does not know how parents would behave, one can conclude only that the graduation rate with an offer of preschool would be between 0.16 and 1.

Both extreme outcomes can occur if parents aim to maximize their children's prospects for high school graduation. Then the graduation rate can be as high as 1 if parents have full knowledge of treatment response. It can be as low as 0.16 if parents completely misperceive treatment response and, as a consequence, make uniformly wrong preschool decisions for their children.

To understand this result, we need to be clear about what classical experimental evidence does and does not reveal. First, a classical experiment that compels or prohibits enrollment does not reveal anything about how parents would behave when offered the opportunity to enroll their children. Second, the experiment only partially identifies the distribution of treatment response.

To see precisely what an experiment does reveal about treatment response, observe that each child has a pair of potential high-school graduation outcomes: (graduation without preschool, graduation with preschool). Let the outcome equal one if a child were to graduate and zero if not. There are four possible response patterns: (0, 0), (0, 1), (1, 0), (1, 1). A child has response (0, 0) if he would not graduate regardless of treatment, response (0, 1) if he would not graduate under treatment A but would graduate under treatment B, and so on.

Let $F(0, 0)$ be the fraction of children with response pattern (0, 0), let $F(0, 1)$ be the fraction with pattern (0, 1), and so on. Observing the outcomes of the Perry Preschool treatment group reveals that the high school graduation rate would be 0.67 with mandatory enrollment in preschool. This means that $F(0, 1)$ and $F(1, 1)$ add up to 0.67, while $F(0, 0)$ and $F(1, 0)$ add up to 0.33. Observing the outcomes of the control group reveals that the high school graduation rate would be 0.49 in the absence of preschool. This means that $F(1, 0)$ and $F(1, 1)$ add up to 0.49, while $F(0, 0)$ and $F(0, 1)$ add up to 0.51. Summarizing this information, the experiment reveals that

$$F(0, 1) + F(1, 1) = 0.67, \ F(0, 0) + F(1, 0) = 0.33,$$
$$F(1, 0) + F(1, 1) = 0.49, \ F(0, 0) + F(0, 1) = 0.51.$$

Children with response pattern $(1, 1)$ graduate from high school regardless of treatment. Those with pattern $(0, 0)$ do not graduate regardless of treatment. Treatment only affects those with patterns $(0, 1)$ and $(1, 0)$. The larger the fractions of children with the latter patterns, the greater the potential impact of parental treatment choice on the graduation rate.

Among all frequency distributions that are consistent with the experimental evidence, the one that makes the fractions $F(0, 1)$ and $F(1, 0)$ as large as possible can be shown to be

$$F(0, 0) = 0 \qquad F(1, 0) = 0.33$$
$$F(0, 1) = 0.51 \qquad F(1, 1) = 0.16.$$

Given this distribution of treatment response, the graduation rate is maximized if parents of children with response pattern $(0, 1)$ choose to enroll their children in preschool and parents of children with pattern $(1, 0)$ choose not to enroll them. That is, parents always act to maximize their children's graduation outcomes. The result is a 100 percent graduation rate.

At the other extreme, the graduation probability is minimized if parents of children with response pattern $(0, 1)$ choose not to enroll their children and parents of children with pattern $(1, 0)$ do enroll them. That is, whether driven by preference or by misperception of treatment response, parents always act to minimize their children's graduation outcomes. The result is a 16 percent graduation rate, the only graduates in this case being children with the $(1, 1)$ response pattern.

Social Interactions

The assumption of individualistic response has been pervasive in analysis of treatment response, but there often is ample reason to question its realism. I earlier cited vaccination against infectious disease as an obvious case. I could have raised the possibility of interactions when discussing various other policy problems as well.

For example, programs aiming to help unemployed workers find jobs may affect not only the employment of program participants but also that of nonparticipants. The social mechanism is competition in the labor market. Economists think of employment as the outcome of the interaction of workers and employers, with workers offering to supply labor and employers offering to hire workers. Suppose that a job training program or an intervention such as the Illinois wage subsidy succeeds in making participants more attractive to employers. Then it is reasonable to expect that participants become more likely to receive job offers than otherwise, while the job prospects of nonparticipants diminish.

Local and Global Interactions

Analysis of treatment response with social interactions is a complex subject. Persons may interact in many ways. Researchers may entertain myriad assumptions about these interactions. In this space, I will only draw the important distinction between *local* and *global* interactions. Randomized experiments can identify treatment response in the former case but not the latter.

The classical argument for random assignment of treatments assumes a large population within which treatment is individualistic. However, the argument does not specify the nature of the "individuals" who make up the population. In the policy illustrations that I have given so far, the treatment units have been persons. The argument for randomization applies equally well if the population partitions into a large number of symmetric reference groups of persons. Symmetry here means that the members of each group interact with one another but not with the members of other groups. Reference groups might be households, school classrooms, or neighborhoods. In each of these and similar cases, we can conceptualize the treatment units as reference groups, the policy problem as choice of reference-group treatments, and identify treatment response by randomly assigning treatments to reference groups. Interactions of this type are *local*.

Social interactions are *global* if all members of a population potentially interact with each another. Thus, the population comprises a single reference group. A randomized experiment has no predictive power when interactions are global. Any treatment assignment process, randomized or other, yields exactly one realized collection of treatments for the population. Unless one has knowledge that restricts the nature of interactions, it is impossible to predict the outcomes that would occur under any counterfactual collection of population treatments. In principle, varying the treatment received by just one person could arbitrarily change the outcomes of all population members.

Credible Analysis of Experimental Data

For the above and other reasons, randomized experiments in practice often differ materially from the ideal symbolized by the "gold standard." Serious researchers have long recognized this. Although I criticized Donald Campbell in Chapter 1 for elevating internal validity above external validity, I should make clear that Campbell recognized many of the problems that experiments may face in practice. Campbell and Stanley (1963), a book that has been something of a bible to many social scientists concerned with program evaluation, discussed various "factors jeopardizing the validity" of experiments.

In the economics literature, extrapolation and compliance were prominent concerns of researchers analyzing data from the negative income tax and welfare experiments of the 1970s and 1980s. Many of the contributors to the volumes edited by Hausman and Wise (1985) and Manski and Garfinkel (1992) concluded that researchers must face up to these issues if they are to offer credible predictions of policy outcomes.

What can randomized experiments credibly reveal in practice? Some analysts advocating experiments offer no guidance beyond the platitude that one should design them carefully. Many experimental evaluations of social programs are silent on the problem of extrapolating from the experiments performed to the policies of interest. A prominent example, mentioned earlier in Chapter 1, is the influential set of analyses of welfare reform experiments reported in Gueron and Pauly (1991).

I think it more constructive to explicitly recognize the respects in which experiments may not adhere to the classical ideal and to study inference in these circumstances. Even if an experiment does not yield credible certitude about policy outcomes, it may enable credible interval predictions. My analyses earlier in this section of compliance and the mixing problem illustrate the possibilities.

2.7. Random Treatment Choice in Observational Studies

When introducing the assumption of identical treatment groups, I wrote that this assumption is often suspect in observational studies. Nevertheless, researchers performing observational studies often assume that the treatment groups produced by purposeful treatment choice have identical response distributions.

When analysts feel uncomfortable assuming that complete treatment groups respond identically, they often divide the study population into groups who share specified characteristics, commonly called *covariates*. They then assume that groups who share the same covariates but receive different treatments have the same distribution of treatment response. Essentially, they interpret the outcome data as if they were produced by a series of covariate-specific randomized experiments.

To motivate the assumption that treatment is random within specified groups, researchers often say that dividing the population into groups sharing the same covariates "controls for" treatment choice. However, they do not explain what they have in mind by the expression "controls for." They may, perhaps, think that persons with the same observed characteristics are identical specimens, as in the controlled experiments of the natural sciences. However, if they really were identical, all persons who have the same covariates and receive the same treatment should experience the same outcome. This demonstrably does not occur in practice. The norm is to observe heterogeneous outcomes.

Unfortunately, justifications for assuming random assignment within groups rarely go beyond loose statements that covariates "control for" treatment choice. Consider, for example, judicial sentencing of offenders. Researchers often divide offenders into groups defined by sex, age, race, and/or prior offense record. They assume that judicial choice of treatment is random within each group, but offer no knowledge of judicial behavior to support the assumption.

Judges may base sentencing decisions in part on case characteristics that analysts typically do not observe—from the testimony of witnesses to the demeanor of offenders. The distribution of treatment response may vary with these characteristics. If so, there is no good reason to think that treatment selection is random within the groups defined by characteristics that analysts observe. Smith and Paternoster (1990, 1111–1112) cautioned criminologists about this:

> High risk youth are more likely to receive more severe dispositions. Thus, those individuals assigned more severe sanctions would be more likely to commit new offenses whether or not any relationship existed between juvenile court disposition and future offending.

They went on to argue that it is implausible to assume that judicial treatment choice is random conditional on the covariates that researchers typically can observe.

Rational Treatment Choice and Selection Bias

Within the broad scientific community concerned with policy analysis, economists have been especially skeptical of research assuming that purposeful treatment choice yields identical treatment groups. Economists commonly view choice as a rational activity, in which a decision maker evaluates the merits of alternative actions and selects the one that appears most promising. Applying this basic idea, economists assume that the decision maker first seeks to predict the outcomes of alternative treatments and then chooses the treatment with the best perceived prospects.

It often is reasonable to expect some overlap between the outcomes of concern to decision makers choosing treatments and those of interest in policy analysis. If so, and if decision makers have some ability to predict outcomes, then treatment choice ordinarily will not yield identical treatment groups. Instead, the distribution of treatment response within the group receiving treatment *A* will differ from the response distribution in the group receiving *B*. This phenomenon is sometimes called *selection bias*.

Outcome Optimization with Perfect Foresight

Selection bias is particularly evident under an economic model that makes two assumptions. First, the decision makers in the study population aim to choose treatments that maximize the outcome of interest in policy analysis. Second, these decision makers have full knowledge of treatment response, an assumption called *perfect foresight*. Heckman and

Taber (2008) remark that outcome optimization with perfect foresight is "one of the most important models in economics." They call it the *Roy Model*, referencing its early application to the study of occupation choice and earnings by the British economist A. D. Roy (Roy 1951).

Consider, for example, choice among medical treatments. The decision makers might be physicians. The outcome of common concern to physicians and society might be patient life spans. Then outcome optimization with perfect foresight assumes that physicians know the survival outcomes of alternative treatments and choose ones yielding the longest life spans.

Or consider judicial sentencing of offenders. The decision makers are judges. The outcome of common concern to judges and society might be recidivism. Then outcome optimization with perfect foresight assumes that judges know the consequences of alternative sentences and choose ones that minimize future criminality.

The model of outcome optimization with perfect foresight makes such strong assumptions that I do not take it seriously as a realistic description of treatment choice. It may sometimes be reasonable to assume that the outcome of concern to decision makers choosing treatments for the study population is the same as the outcome of policy interest. However, it is hard to see how these decision makers could possess complete knowledge of treatment response, when policy analysts struggle to achieve even partial knowledge.

The model nonetheless provides a useful illustration of how selection bias may arise. Whatever the context may be, outcome optimization with perfect foresight implies that the groups of treatment units that receive treatments A and B have different distributions of treatment response. Treatment A yields a better outcome than B within the group receiving treatment A. Symmetrically, B yields a better outcome than A within the group receiving B.

Regression Discontinuity Analysis

Perhaps the best case for assuming that treatment choice is random conditional on observed covariates has been made in occasional settings where an institutional process is known to use only observed covariates to assign persons to treatment. Then it is sometimes reasonable to assume that groups who have similar covariates but receive different treatments have similar distributions of treatment response.

The idea was introduced by Thistlethwaite and Campbell (1960), who compared some outcomes experienced by two groups of high school students who were judged to be similar but who received different treatments. The members of both groups were strong academic achievers who performed well in a national scholarship competition. Students in one group received considerable public recognition in the form of a certificate of merit, while those in the other group received lesser recognition in the form of a personal letter of commendation. The institutional decision to give a certificate of merit or a letter of commendation was based mainly on scores on a standardized test. Students with test scores above a threshold received the certificate, and those with scores slightly below the threshold received the letter.

Thistlethwaite and Campbell focused on two groups of students with scores close to the threshold. One group, with scores slightly above the threshold, received the certificate. The other, with scores slightly below the threshold, received the letter. The authors judged that the two groups were similar in composition, reasoning that attainment of a score slightly above or below the threshold reflected essentially random differences in test performance rather than underlying differences in student quality. Given this, the authors analyzed the outcomes of the two treatment groups as if treatments had been assigned randomly.

They used the term *regression-discontinuity analysis* to describe their idea. The explanation for this term is that an analyst estimating the regression of outcomes on test scores would ordinarily expect to find that outcomes tend to vary smoothly with test scores. (The regression of outcomes on test scores measures how average outcomes vary across groups with different test scores.) However, the use of a test-score threshold to assign treatment might yield a discontinuity in outcomes at the threshold, as persons above and below the threshold receive different treatments. The magnitude of this discontinuity measures the average effect of receiving one treatment rather than the other.

Regression discontinuity analysis has since been applied in various educational and other settings where institutional rules determine treatments. For example, Angrist and Krueger (1991) used it to study outcomes when children are subjected to different numbers of years of compulsory schooling. They described their analysis in the abstract to their article (p. 979):

> We establish that season of birth is related to educational attainment because of school start age policy and compulsory school attendance laws. Individuals born in the beginning of the year start school at an older age, and can therefore drop out after completing less schooling than individuals born near the end of the year.

Here the treatment is the number of years that a child is subject to compulsory schooling. The observed covariate determining treatment is date of birth. The threshold determining treatment is the birth date (often January 1) used to determine when compulsory schooling begins. Children born just before the threshold date are required to attend school for close to one year longer than children born just after the threshold. Reasoning that exact birth dates are essentially random, the authors analyzed the schooling and earnings outcomes of children born just before and after the threshold date as if they were randomly assigned to different numbers of years of compulsory schooling.

In the above and other applications where observable institutional processes determine treatments, researchers often judge regression discontinuity analysis to be highly credible. An important limitation of the idea is that it enables one to predict only the outcomes of rather specific policies, and then only for groups with particular covariate values. Thistlethwaite and Campbell were only able to compare outcomes given receipt of a certificate of merit or a letter of commendation, and then only for students with test scores near the treatment threshold. Angrist and Krueger were only able to compare outcomes for one-year differences in the period of compulsory schooling, and then only for students with birth dates near the treatment threshold.

2.8. Modeling Rational Treatment Choice

I observed in Section 2.7 that the economic view of treatment choice as a rational activity regularly casts doubt that treatment choice in study populations is random conditional on observed covariates. One might therefore expect economists performing observational studies to be cautious in predicting policy outcomes. This has not been the case. Economists have been at least as prone to incredible certitude as other policy analysts, perhaps more so. To predict policy outcomes without assuming identical treatment groups, economists have developed *selection models* that relate treatment choice and treatment response.

The archetypical selection model assumes outcome optimization with perfect foresight. I said earlier that this model makes such strong assumptions that I do not take it seriously as a realistic description of treatment choice. It may therefore be surprising to learn that, despite the strength of its assumptions, the model does not yield point-predictions of policy outcomes.

Outcome Optimization as a Model of Sentencing

To show what inference the model does enable, I will again discuss the Manski and Nagin (1998) analysis of sentencing and recidivism in Utah. When considering sentencing and recidivism in Section 2.3, I assumed nothing about how judges make sentencing decisions. Now assume that judges can perfectly predict outcomes and that they choose sentences to minimize recidivism.

As earlier, consider prediction of the outcomes that would occur if all offenders were to receive treatment B (confinement). The problem is that outcomes under B are unobservable for offenders who actually received treatment A (non-confinement). We previously could say nothing about these counterfactual outcomes. With the assumption of outcome optimization with perfect foresight, we can draw partial conclusions about them. Specifically, the counterfactual recidivism outcomes can be no better than the observed outcomes. The reason is that if outcomes under treatment B were better than under A, judges would have chosen B rather than A.

This reasoning yields a tighter lower bound on R_{MB} than was derived earlier in Section 2.3. The lower bound previously was $R_B \times F_B$. Now it is the observed recidivism rate under the status quo policy, namely $R_A \times F_A + R_B \times F_B$. The outcome optimization model yields no implications for the upper bound on recidivism. Hence, the revised bound is

$$R_A \times F_A + R_B \times F_B \leq R_{MB} \leq F_A + R_B \times F_B.$$

Numerically, the lower bound previously was 0.08. Now it is 0.61. The upper bound remains 0.97.

Distributional Assumptions

The above derivation shows that the assumption of outcome optimization and perfect foresight has predictive power, but not enough to yield point predictions of policy outcomes. Nevertheless, economists using the model routinely report point predictions. How so?

To achieve certitude, economists combine the model with *distributional assumptions* that sharply constrain the population distribution of treatment response. In the 1970s, econometricians showed that imposing certain distributional assumptions enables one to fully determine the outcomes that would occur under policies that mandate specified treatments. They also showed that, given strong enough distributional assumptions, prediction with certitude remains possible if one weakens the assumptions of outcome optimization and perfect foresight to some extent. The formal arguments used to obtain point predictions do not have intuitive explanations, so I will not try to describe them here. Interested readers with sufficient background in econometrics or statistics can find a clear technical exposition in the monograph of Maddala (1983).

Many economists have and continue to use selection models to predict policy outcomes, with especially widespread application of a computationally simple "two-step" method for estimation of certain models (Heckman 1976, 1979). However, this approach to analysis of treatment response has long been controversial. The reason is a severe lack of credibility.

The conventional two-step method assumes a *normal-linear model* of treatment response. Here the outcomes of treatments *A* and *B* are continuous variables whose frequency distribution among persons with specified covariates is assumed to have the shape of a bivariate normal distribution. The mean response of persons with different covariates is assumed to vary linearly as a function of the covariates, while the variance of response is assumed not to vary with covariates.

These are technical assumptions of convenience, made to enable point prediction but lacking substantive justification. It is therefore not surprising that many researchers question the credibility of the normal-linear model and, hence, distrust analyses that use the model. Indeed, criticism of the normal-linear model figured prominently in the recommendation by Bassi and Ashenfelter (1986) and LaLonde (1986), cited earlier, that study of treatment response should focus exclusively on the design and analysis of randomized experiments.

3

——◦◦◦◦——

Predicting Behavior

THIS chapter continues to study prediction of policy outcomes, addressing problems more challenging than those examined in Chapter 2. Again the problem is to predict the outcomes that would occur under a policy mandating some treatment. The fresh challenge is that the data come from a study population in which no one received the treatment that would be mandated. For example, in the context of sentencing and recidivism, we may have data on outcomes under a policy where no juveniles were sentenced to confinement and we may want to predict the outcomes that would occur if all were confined. Thus, we may want to predict the outcomes of an entirely new treatment.

The two identical-response assumptions studied in Chapter 2—identical treatment units and identical treatment groups—have no power to predict the outcomes of a new treatment. If everyone in the study population received one treatment, these assumptions reveal nothing about what would happen if someone were to receive another treatment. How then might one proceed?

A broad idea not used in Chapter 2 is to make assumptions about how individuals respond to treatment. Such assumptions, combined with observation of the study population, can yield conclusions about the outcomes that would occur if persons were to receive the new treatment. Economists have long used this idea to predict behavioral response to new policy, referring to their work as *revealed preference analysis*.

When predicting behavioral response, a treatment is the collection of choice alternatives available to a person, called the *choice set* for short. Suppose that one observes the choices that members of a study population make when facing status quo choice sets. The problem is to predict the choices that they or others would make when facing different choice sets. Policy operates on persons by affecting the choice sets they face.

Revealed preference analysis was introduced by Paul Samuelson. Samuelson (1938, 1948) considered the classical economic problem of predicting commodity demands. He supposed that a researcher observes the purchases that persons make when incomes and prices take status quo values. He showed that these observations, combined with standard consumer theory, enable partial prediction of the purchases that these persons would make in new income-price settings. Policy may operate on persons by affecting their incomes and/or the prices of commodities.

I will describe modern applications of revealed preference analysis to prediction of policy outcomes and discuss the assumptions that economists have used. I begin with a leading case that has drawn substantial research attention, the response of labor supply to income tax policy.

3.1. Income Taxation and Labor Supply

Prediction of the response of labor supply to income taxation has long been an important concern of economic policy analysis. Income taxation is a central mechanism for generating government revenue. Tax policy may affect labor supply. Tax policy and labor supply together determine earned income and, hence, tax revenue.

Discussion of public finance in the United States has been characterized by dueling certitudes regarding the response of labor supply to income taxation, with opposing beliefs classified as conservative versus liberal. Much debate has centered on the marginal rate of taxation of high income. Conservatives assert that the labor supply of skilled persons would increase significantly if the tax rates applied to high incomes would be reduced relative to those in our progressive taxation system. Liberals assert that the labor supply of skilled persons is relatively insensitive to tax rates.

In the 1980s, a bold version of the conservative assertion came from the economist Arthur Laffer. He maintained that reduction in the marginal rate of taxation of high income would stimulate a sufficiently large increase in skilled labor supply as to increase government tax revenue. Liberals countered that the predictions of Laffer and other "supply-side" economists were wildly inaccurate. The specific arguments made by conservatives and liberals may change over time, but the debate continues.

The Theory of Labor Supply

It is important to understand that standard economic theory does not predict the response of labor supply to income taxation. To the contrary, it shows that a worker may rationally respond in disparate ways. As tax rates increase, a person may rationally decide to work less, work more, or not change his labor supply at all.

Modern labor economics envisions labor supply as a complex sequence of schooling, occupation, and work effort decisions made over the life course. However, a simple model familiar to students of economics suffices to show that a person may respond to income taxes in disparate ways. This model considers a person who has a predetermined wage for paid work. The person must allocate a specified unit of time (perhaps a day, a week, or a month) between paid work and the various nonpaid activities that economists traditionally call leisure. His net income equals his gross income minus his income tax.

Economists generally suppose, as seems reasonable, that persons prefer to have more income and more leisure. The essence of the labor supply problem is that a person cannot simultaneously increase his income and his leisure. Whereas income increases with the amount of time worked, leisure commensurately decreases. Standard economic theory supposes that the person attaches a value, or utility, to each feasible (net income, leisure) pair and chooses his time allocation to maximize utility. Beyond the presumption that net income and leisure are both desirable, theory is silent on the preferences that persons hold.

Economists have found that different preferences imply different relationships between tax policy and labor supply. A simple exercise considers a person with no unearned income and asks how labor supply varies with the tax rate under a proportional tax policy—a policy that taxes each dollar earned at the same rate. Three preference types familiar to students of economics are *additive, Cobb-Douglas,* and *Leontief* utility. Additive and Leontief utility are polar cases, the former viewing income and leisure as perfect substitutes and the latter viewing them as

perfect complements. It can be shown that a person with additive utility chooses to work full time when the tax rate is low and not to work
at all when the tax rate is high. Someone with Leontief utility chooses
to work more as the tax rate rises. Cobb-Douglas utility is an interme-
diate case in which labor supply does not vary with the tax rate.

These three preference types yield very different relationships between the tax rate and labor supply, but they do not exhaust the possibilities. Economics textbooks regularly discuss *backward-bending* labor
supply functions. Labor supply is said to be backward bending if the
fraction of time worked initially increases as net wage rises from zero
but, above some threshold, decreases as net wage rises further. This implies that labor supply initially increases as the tax rate rises from zero
but, above some threshold, decreases as the tax rate rises further. Some
utility functions yield even more-complex relationships between tax
rates and labor supply (see Stern 1986).

Economic theory does not give a privileged status to any particular preferences. Some persons may have additive utility functions, some
Cobb-Douglas, and some Leontief. Others may have preferences that
imply backward-bending labor supply or other relationships between tax
rates and time allocation. Thus, theory does not predict how income
taxation affects labor supply.

Empirical Analysis

The silence of theory has long been appreciated. As early as 1930, the
economist Lionel Robbins recognized this and concluded that prediction
of the response of labor supply to tax policy requires empirical analysis.
Robbins (1930, 129) put it this way: "We are left with the conclusion . . .
that any attempt to predict the effect of a change in the terms on which
income is earned must proceed by inductive investigation of elasticities."
Here the word *inductive* means empirical inference from data, and *elasticities* refers to the percentages by which persons would change their work
time if the tax rate were to increase by 1 percent.

Economists have subsequently performed numerous empirical
studies of labor supply, using two approaches. One approach applies the
assumptions examined in Chapter 2, without reference to the economic theory of labor supply. Researchers may perform before-and-
after studies, comparing labor supply in a given tax jurisdiction before

and after a change in tax policy. Or they may compare the labor supply of persons living in different tax jurisdictions. A basic limitation of such analyses is that historical and geographic variation in tax policies spans only a small subset of the policies that a society may contemplate. The assumptions of Chapter 2 do not enable prediction of labor supply under new tax policies.

The second strand of empirical research studies labor supply through the lens of economic theory. Researchers engaged in revealed preference analysis observe the labor supply decisions made by a study population under a status quo tax policy. To use these data to predict labor supply under new policies, researchers first invoke the standard economic assumption that persons allocate their time to maximize utility. This assumption explains the term *revealed preference.* Economists assume that a person prefers the (net income, leisure) pair he chooses to all other pairs that he could have chosen. Hence, observation of a person's chosen labor supply under the status quo tax policy reveals something about his preferences. This idea originated in Samuelson (1938, 1948).

The assumption of utility maximization per se has little predictive power, so researchers place assumptions on preferences that are strong enough to yield point predictions of behavioral responses to new tax policies. A simple and credible assumption is that persons value both income and leisure—that is, *more is better.* However, this preference assumption at most enables one to bound labor supply under new tax policies. To make point predictions, economists impose much stronger assumptions.

Labor-supply models differ across studies, but they generally share two assumptions. First, they suppose that labor supply varies unidirectionally with net wage. Thus, model specifications do not generally permit backward-bending labor supply functions or other non-monotone relationships. Second, studies usually suppose that the response of labor supply to net wage is identical within broad groups such as prime age males or married females. That is, they assume that all group members would adjust work time in the same way in response to a conjectural change in net wage. To the extent that authors permit heterogeneity in preferences, they impose distributional assumptions similar to those discussed in Section 2.8, made to enable point prediction but lacking substantive justification.

Credibility aside, the practice of revealed preference analysis enables prediction of labor supply under new tax policies. The prediction process has two steps. First, one computes the net income that each time allocation would yield under a contemplated policy. Then one uses the model of labor supply to predict worker decisions.

A large body of such research was stimulated by the work of Burtless and Hausman (1978). The methodologies, data, and findings of the ensuing literature have been summarized and critiqued in multiple lengthy review articles including Pencavel (1986), Killingsworth and Heckman (1986), Blundell and MaCurdy (1999), Meghir and Phillips (2010), Keane (2011), and Saez, Slemrod, and Giertz (2012). The CBO has described its use of the literature to predict labor supply response to tax policy in Congressional Budget Office (1996, 2007).

Attempting to distill the huge literature, Meghir and Phillips write (p. 204):

> Our conclusion is that hours of work do not respond particularly strongly to the financial incentives created by tax changes for men, but they are a little more responsive for married women and lone mothers. On the other hand, the decision whether or not to take paid work at all is quite sensitive to taxation and benefits for women and mothers in particular.

Saez, Slemrod, and Giertz similarly write (p. 1):

> With some exceptions, the profession has settled on a value for this elasticity close to zero for prime-age males, although for married women the responsiveness of labor force participation appears to be significant. Overall, though, the compensated elasticity of labor appears to be fairly small.

Keane expresses a different perspective (p. 1071): "My review suggests that labor supply of men may be more elastic than conventional wisdom suggests."

Reading the recent empirical literature, I have been struck to find that while authors may differ on the magnitude of labor-supply elasticities, they agree on the direction of the effect of taxes on labor supply. Researchers may recognize the theoretical possibility that labor supply may increase with tax rates, but they view this as an empirical rarity. The consensus is that increasing tax rates usually reduces work effort. Considering the effect of a rise in a proportional tax, Meghir and Phillips write (p. 207), "in most cases this will lead to less work, but when the income effect dominates the substitution effect at high hours of work it may increase effort." Keane states the directionality of the effect without reservation (p. 963): "The use of labor income taxation to raise revenue causes people to work less." The view that increasing tax rates reduces labor supply has been accepted in official government forecasts of the response of labor supply to income taxation (see Congressional Budget Office 2007).

Basic Revealed-Preference Analysis

I abstracted from credibility while describing the findings reported in revealed preference analysis of labor supply. I now return to this key issue.

In Manski (2012), I study the predictions yielded by revealed-preference analysis when one strips away the strong assumptions made in the literature and makes only the two most basic assumptions of standard theory: (1) a person chooses his time allocation to maximize utility, and (2) utility increases with income and leisure (more is better). The analysis is too technical to present here, but I can summarize the main findings and illustrate the key idea.

I find that combining the two basic assumptions with observation of a person's time allocation under a status quo tax policy does not yield point predictions of labor supply under new policies—one can at most obtain interval predictions. Moreover, one cannot predict whether labor supply would increase or decrease in response to changes in tax policy. Thus, the sharp findings reported in the literature necessarily require additional assumptions beyond the two basic ones.

I find that a precondition for basic revealed preference analysis to have any predictive power is that the status quo and new tax schedules cross at least once. That is, one policy must yield lower net income than the other at some time allocations but higher net income at other time allocations. This implies that basic analysis has no predictive power when the status quo is a proportional tax and the new policy is a proportional tax at a different rate. On the other hand, the analysis may have some predictive power when one policy is a progressive tax and the other is a proportional tax.

Illustration: Labor Supply under Progressive and Proportional Taxes

To illustrate what basic revealed preference analysis can accomplish, suppose that the status quo is a two-rate progressive schedule that taxes income at a rate of 15 percent up to $50,000 per year and at a rate of 25 percent above $50,000. Consider a new proportional policy that taxes all income at a rate of 20 percent. The two tax schedules cross when gross annual income equals $100,000, where both take $20,000 in tax and yield net income of $80,000. The status quo schedule yields more net income than the new one when gross income is under $100,000 and less when it is over $100,000.

Figure 3.1 shows how net income varies with time allocation under both policies for a person with no unearned income whose gross annual income for full-time work is $150,000. This person earns net income of $80,000 under both policies if he works ⅔ of the year and takes ⅓ as leisure. The new policy yields higher net income than the status quo if he takes less than ⅓ time as leisure and lower net income than the status quo if he take more than ⅓ time leisure.

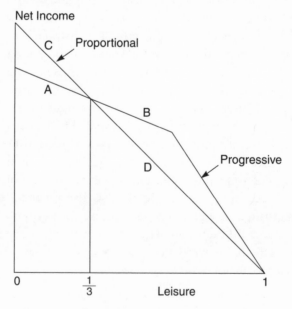

Figure 3.1: Net income with progressive and proportional tax schedules

Consider a person who is observed under the status quo policy to take less than $1/3$ time leisure. Basic revealed preference analysis shows that he would continue to take less than $1/3$ time leisure under the new policy. To see this, suppose for concreteness that the person is observed to work $4/5$ time under the status quo policy and take $1/5$ time as leisure. Let us compare this with the alternative of working half time. Under the status quo, working $4/5$ time yields the (net income, leisure) pair ($95,000, $1/5$) shown as point A in the figure, and working half time yields ($61,250, $1/2$) shown as point B. Under the new policy, working $4/5$ time yields ($96,000, $1/5$) and working half time yields ($60,000, $1/2$), shown as points C and D respectively.

Observation that the person chose to work $4/5$ time under the status quo coupled with the assumption of utility maximization implies that he prefers (net income, leisure) point A to B. The assumption that more is better implies that he prefers C to A and that he prefers B to D. Combining these findings implies that he prefers C to D. Thus, if the new tax policy were imposed, he would prefer to work $4/5$ time over working half time.

The same reasoning applies when the person is observed to take anything less than $1/3$ time leisure and the alternative is to take anything more than $1/3$ time leisure. However, I show in Manski (2012) that basic revealed preference analysis does not yield any further conclusions.

3.2. Discrete Choice Analysis

The illustration just given applies Samuelson's original version of revealed preference analysis, which aims to predict the choice behavior of an individual. Modern economic policy analysis mainly applies ideas that took shape in work of Daniel McFadden (1974). He developed a form of revealed preference analysis that seeks to predict the distribution of choices made by the members of a population with heterogeneous preferences. His framework has four essential features. I will explain and then give an illustration.

Random Utility Model Representation of Behavior

McFadden supposed that a researcher observes the decisions made by a study population, each member of which faces a *discrete choice* problem.

A discrete choice problem is simply one in which the decision maker chooses among a finite set of alternatives. For example, persons might choose among three options for time allocation—full-time, half-time, or no work. Discrete choice analysis aims to predict the behavior of populations who face such choice problems.

We begin with the standard economic assumption that each person makes the best choice among the available alternatives; that is, he maximizes utility. A *random utility model* expresses the idea that the fraction of persons who choose a particular alternative equals the fraction of persons who prefer this alternative to all others. The fraction of persons who choose a particular alternative is called its *choice probability.*

In psychology, random utility models date back to Thurstone (1927) as a way of conceptualizing semi-rational behavior. The psychological interpretation, exposited in Luce and Suppes (1965), assumes that each decision maker carries a distribution of utility functions in his head and selects one at random whenever a decision must be made. McFadden reinterpreted the randomness as arising from variation in utility functions across the population rather than variation within an individual.

Attribute Representation of Alternatives and Decision Makers

Discrete choice analysis aims to predict behavior in counterfactual settings where new alternatives become available, existing ones become unavailable, or new decision makers arise. This is achieved by describing alternatives and persons as bundles of attributes. With knowledge of these attributes and the form of a person's utility function, a researcher can determine the utility of any alternative to any decision maker and hence can predict the decision maker's choice behavior. For example, a transportation researcher can predict how commuters with specified income and job attributes would choose among travel modes with specified travel-time and travel-cost attributes.

Description of alternatives and decision makers as bundles of attributes marked a sharp departure from prevailing economic practice. In classical consumer theory, commodities are qualitatively distinct and so are consumers. There is no way to predict the demand for a new commodity. Nor is there any way to predict the behavior of new consumers.

Analysis with Incomplete Attribute Data

It is not realistic to think that an empirical researcher will have complete data on the attributes of persons and the alternatives available to them. Nor is it realistic to think that the researcher fully knows the form of the utility functions that express preferences. Random utility models do not ignore the possible effects of unobserved attributes on behavior. They formally treat the unobserved attributes of decision makers as variables whose unknown values may vary across the study population. They treat the unobserved attributes of alternatives as variables whose unknown values may vary across alternatives.

Practicality

Discrete choice analysis aims to be a practical prediction method. Mc-Fadden judged that, with the computational technology available at the time of his work, analysis would be computationally tractable only if choice probabilities have a simple form. With this in mind, he searched for a convenient distributional assumption to impose on the unobserved attributes. He found one that yielded the highly tractable *conditional logit* model, which has been used in numerous empirical studies. This model associates a certain utility index with each alternative and predicts that, among persons with common observed attributes, the fraction who choose a specified alternative is the utility index of this alternative divided by the sum of the indices of all alternatives in the choice set.

College Choice in America

I shall use a highly simplified version of my own early analysis of college-going behavior, performed with David Wise, to illustrate application of the conditional logit model. Manski and Wise (1983, chaps. 6, 7) used data from a survey of American youth in the high school class of 1972 to estimate a random utility model of college enrollment. We used the estimated model to predict the enrollment impacts of the Pell Grant program, the major federal college scholarship program.

The starting point for our analysis was to assume that the patterns of college enrollment and labor force participation observed among the survey respondents are the consequence of decisions made by these students, by colleges, and by employers. Colleges and employers make admissions decisions and job offers that determine the options available to each high school senior upon graduation. Each senior selects among the available options.

What do the available survey data reveal about the decision processes generating postsecondary activities? If we assume that a student chooses the most preferred alternative from the available options, observations of chosen activities partially reveal student preferences. For simplicity, assume that after high school graduation a student has two alternatives: college enrollment and work. (The model actually estimated posed multiple schooling and work alternatives.) If we observe that a person chose to go to college, we can infer that the utility of college enrollment exceeds that of working. If the person chose to work, then the opposite inequality holds. The survey data provide a large set of these inequalities, one for each respondent.

The preference inequalities implied by observation of actual activity choices do not provide enough information to allow one to predict how a student not in the sample would select between college and work, nor how a student in the sample would have behaved if conditions had differed. To extrapolate behavior, we must combine the data with assumptions restricting the form of preferences.

For example, we might assume that the utility of college enrollment depends in a particular way on a student's ability and parents' income, on the quality and net tuition of her best college option, and on unobserved attributes of the student and her best college option. Similarly, the utility of working might depend on the wage and unobserved attributes of the best work option.

Predicting the Enrollment Effects of Student Aid Policy

Manski and Wise (1983) estimated a model that is considerably more complex than the one described above, but not qualitatively different. The estimated model was used to study the impact on freshman college enrollments of the Basic Educational Opportunity Grant program, later renamed the Pell Grant program. This federal scholarship program was initiated in 1973, so members of the high school class of 1972 were not eligible at the time of their initial postsecondary schooling decisions.

Table 3.1   Predicted enrollments in 1979, with and without the
Pell Grant program (thousands of students)

Income group	All schools		Four-year college		Two-year college		Voc-tech school	
	with Pell	without Pell	with Pell	without Pell	with Pell	without Pell	with Pell	without Pell
Lower	590	370	128	137	349	210	113	23
Middle	398	354	162	164	202	168	34	22
Upper	615	600	377	378	210	198	28	24
Total	1603	1324	668	679	761	576	174	69

Lower income = below $16,900. Upper income = above $21,700.
Source: Manski and Wise (1983), table 7.4.

In the context of our model, the Pell Grant program influences behavior by changing the college net tuition that students face. Given knowledge of the program eligibility criteria and award formula, we can estimate the net tuition of college to any given student in the presence of the program. This done, we can predict how students would behave in the presence and absence of the program. We can then aggregate these predictions to generate predictions of aggregate freshman college enrollments in the United States.

Table 3.1 presents our findings concerning the version of the program in effect in 1979. The predictions indicate that the Pell Grant program was responsible for a substantial increase (59 percent) in the college enrollment rate of low-income students, a moderate increase (12 percent) in middle-income enrollments, and a minor increase (3 percent) in the rate for upper-income students.

Overall, we predicted that 1,603,000 of the 3,300,000 persons who were high school seniors in 1979 would enroll in full-time postsecondary education in 1979–1980. In contrast, only 1,324,000 would have enrolled had the Pell Grant program not been in operation. The table indicates that the enrollment increases induced by the existence of the program were totally concentrated at two-year colleges and vocational-technical schools. Enrollments at four-year schools were essentially unaffected.

Power and Price of the Analysis

Federal scholarship programs with varying eligibility criteria and award formulae have been proposed, but only a few programs have actually been implemented. Revealed preference analysis of college enrollments makes it possible to predict the enrollment outcomes of a wide variety of proposed and actual programs. This ability to extrapolate is very powerful.

The price of extrapolation is the set of assumptions imposed. The assumption of rational choice alone has very little predictive power. Revealed preference analysis yields strong conclusions only when strong assumptions are placed on preferences and when the researcher assumes that he can suitably describe the choices made by and alternatives available to decision makers.

The Manski-Wise analysis of college choice illustrates the kinds of assumptions that have typically been imposed in empirical studies. When I performed this research in the early 1980s, I felt comfortable reporting the point predictions of table 3.1. Observe that the predictions made in the table were expressed with certitude. I now view them as instances of wishful extrapolation.

Discrete Choice Analysis Today

Since the 1970s, discrete choice analysis has retained the basic aspects of McFadden's original work—the random utility model, the attribute description of alternatives and decision makers, and the resulting choice probabilities. However, the particular distributional assumptions of the conditional logit model have been subjected to close examination, and models making many alternative assumptions have been studied and applied.

The objective of a considerable body of econometric research has been to make assumptions that are less rigid than those of the conditional logit model and yet strong enough to yield point predictions of choice probabilities in new settings. There is an inherent tension between these aims. I describe various streams of the literature in Manski (2007a, chap. 13). I have recently begun to study weaker assumptions that do not yield point predictions but may yield informative interval predictions (see Manski 2007b, 2012).

3.3. Predicting Behavior under Uncertainty

Our discussion of revealed preference analysis has thus far supposed that decision makers have complete knowledge of their choice environments. However, just as researchers may have difficulty predicting policy outcomes, ordinary people may have difficulty predicting the outcomes of their choices. For example, persons deciding labor supply may not know how much they will earn for paid work. Youth choosing among colleges may not know how well they will perform should they enroll in different programs.

When studying behavior under uncertainty, economists have assumed that persons predict the outcomes of making alternative choices and use these predictions to make decisions. It has been particularly common to assume that persons have *rational expectations*. This use of the term "rational" means that persons correctly perceive their choice environments and make the best outcome predictions possible given the information available to them. It should not be confused with the term "rational choice," which means that a person orders alternatives in terms of preference and chooses one that is ranked highest among those that are feasible.

Operationally, economists assume that persons assess the probability that a given action will yield each of various possible outcomes. Going further, they assume that persons use their probabilistic beliefs to form the expected value of the utility of taking each feasible action and that persons choose actions that maximize expected utility. When the probabilities that persons attach to outcomes are simply viewed as personal beliefs, they are called *subjective probabilities*. When subjective probabilities are assumed to be objectively correct, they are called rational expectations. We previously discussed the extreme form of rational expectations in Section 2.7 under the heading *perfect foresight*. Perfect foresight means that persons predict outcomes with certitude and that their predictions are correct.

The assumptions that persons have rational expectations and maximize expected utility help economists predict behavior, but at a potentially high cost in credibility. I will give two illustrations here that call into question the assumption of rational expectations. The next section will discuss the assumption that persons maximize expected utility and the assumption of rational choice more broadly.

How Do Youth Infer the Returns to Schooling?

Consider youth making schooling decisions. Economists suppose that youth predict their personal returns to schooling and that youth use these predictions to choose between schooling and other options. Economists use the term *returns to schooling* to describe comparisons of the life outcomes generated by allocating time to schooling relative to those generated by an alternative use of time, such as working. Empirical studies of schooling decisions regularly assume that youth form rational expectations for the returns to schooling.

The credibility of rational expectations in this context is highly suspect. Labor economists have performed a multitude of empirical studies of the returns to schooling, usually comparing the labor market earnings that follow schooling and other uses of time. Reading this large literature reveals that researchers vary greatly in their assumptions and findings. Youth confront the same inferential problems as do labor economists studying the returns to schooling. If economists have not been able to reach consensus on the returns to schooling, is it plausible that youth have rational expectations? I think not.

I would particularly stress that youth and labor economists alike must contend with the unobservability of counterfactual outcomes. Much as economists attempt to infer the returns to schooling from data on schooling choices and outcomes, youth may attempt to learn through observation of the outcomes experienced by family, friends, and others who have made their own past schooling decisions. However, youth cannot observe the outcomes that these people would have experienced had they made other decisions. The possibilities for inference, and the implications for decision making, depend fundamentally on the assumptions that youth maintain about these counterfactual outcomes. See Manski (1993) for further discussion.

How Do Potential Criminals Perceive Sanctions Regimes?

Stimulated by the work of Gary Becker (1968), economists have assumed that persons contemplating criminal activity make rational choices that maximize expected utility. They have, moreover, assumed that persons have rational expectations regarding the outcomes of crime commission. Non-economists may well question the assumption of rational criminal choice. Even orthodox economists should question the assumption of rational expectations.

A standard economic model supposes that persons place utilities on successful commission of a crime and on failure. Failure may bring arrest, conviction, and sentencing following conviction. Economists assume that persons place subjective probabilities on the spectrum of possible outcomes and commit crimes if doing so yields higher expected utility than not doing so. It has been common to assume that persons have rational expectations, correctly perceiving the probability of a successful criminal outcome and the probability of being sanctioned in various ways through arrest, conviction, and sentencing.

The realism of rational-expectations assumptions may be particularly questionable in studies of the deterrent effect of the death penalty. Suppose for the sake of discussion that persons do weigh the expected benefits and costs of murder. Even accepting this premise, researchers know essentially nothing about how persons form beliefs regarding their chances of arrest, conviction, receipt of a death sentence, and execution of the sentence. The conventional research practice has been to obtain historical data on murders and executions, use them to form frequency rates of execution, and assume that potential murderers use these frequencies as subjective probabilities. This practice has been criticized severely in the National Research Council report of the Committee on Deterrence and the Death Penalty (2012).

Measuring Expectations

In the above illustrations and elsewhere, it is difficult to see why assumptions of rational expectations should have much credibility. To better cope with the difficulty of revealed preference analysis of behavior under uncertainty, one might anticipate that economists would interview persons and ask them to state the expectations they actually hold. However, economists were long deeply skeptical of subjective statements, often asserting that one should believe only what people do, not what they say. As a result, the profession for many years enforced something of a prohibition on the collection of expectations data.

This prohibition began to break down in the early 1990s. Since then, economists engaged in survey research have increasingly asked respondents to report probabilistic expectations of significant personal events. Expectations have been elicited for macroeconomic events (e.g., stock market returns), for risks that a person faces (e.g., job loss, crime victimization, mortality), for future income (e.g., the earnings returns to schooling, Social Security benefits), and for choices that persons make (e.g., durable purchases and voting choices). The review article of Manski (2004a) describes the emergence of this field of empirical research and summarizes a range of applications. Hurd (2009) and Delavande, Giné, and McKenzie (2011) subsequently review additional parts of the now large literature.

Pill, Patch, or Shot?

Delavande (2008) nicely demonstrates the use of research measuring expectations in discrete choice analysis. Delavande studied women's choice of contraception methods in an article titled "Pill, Patch, or Shot?" She assumed that women base their decisions on their beliefs regarding method-related outcomes, including pregnancy and contraction of a sexually transmitted disease (STD).

Rather than make assumptions about expectations, Delavande surveyed women and asked them to state their beliefs about the chance of becoming pregnant or contracting an STD if they were to use alternative contraceptive methods. She then combined the measured expectations with data on contraceptive behavior to estimate a conditional logit model of choice of contraceptive method. The availability of expectations data made it possible for her to identify preferences more persuasively than if she had made unfounded assumptions about expectations. Finally, she used the measured expectations and the estimated choice model to predict contraceptive use in new settings where the prices of contraceptives may change or new methods may become available.

3.4. Perspectives on Rational Choice

I have not yet questioned the basic assumption of rational choice that economists regularly maintain when studying behavior. This standard assumption has long been controversial outside the community of orthodox economists. Psychologists, as well some researchers who call themselves *behavioral economists,* have stressed that humans are organisms with limited perceptual and cognitive powers. This being so, they assert that humans can at most approximate the type of behavior assumed in economic models. Perspectives have differed on the nature and quality of the approximation.

This concluding section comments on the history of thought. I focus more on the arguments that have been made and the kinds of research performed than on the specific findings reported. To organize the discussion, I find it useful to begin in the middle of the twentieth century and move forward from there. The material in this section draws substantially on Manski (2007a, chap. 15).

As-If Rationality

Orthodox economists have long asserted that economic models of maximizing behavior are successful "as if" approximations, even if not literal descriptions of decision processes. This assertion was made particularly strongly by Milton Friedman and Leonard Savage in Friedman and Savage (1948). They defended not just the basic idea of rational choice but the much more specific assumptions that persons maximize expected utility and have rational expectations. One passage in their article, which uses an expert pool player as a metaphor, is so forceful and has been so controversial that I think it useful to quote it in full (p. 298):

> The hypothesis does not assert that individuals explicitly or consciously calculate and compare expected utilities. Indeed, it is not at all clear what such an assertion would mean or how it could be tested. The hypothesis asserts rather that, in making a particular class of decisions, individuals behave *as if* they calculated and compared expected utility and *as if* they knew the odds. The validity of this assertion does not depend on whether individuals know the precise odds, much less on whether they say that they calculate and compare expected utilities or think that they do, or whether it appears to others that they do, or whether psychologists can uncover any evidence that they do, but solely on whether it yields sufficiently accurate predictions about the class of decisions with which the hypothesis deals. Stated differently, the test by results is the only possible method of determining whether the *as if* statement is or is not a sufficiently good approximation to reality for the purpose at hand.

A simple example may help to clarify the point at issue. Consider the problem of predicting, before each shot, the direction of travel of a billiard ball hit by an expert billiard player. It would be possible to construct one or more mathematical formulas that would give the directions of travel that would score points and, among these, would indicate the one (or more) that would leave the balls in the best positions. The formulas might, of course, be extremely complicated, since they would necessarily take account of the location of the balls in relation to one another and to the cushions and of the complicated phenomena introduced by "english." Nonetheless, it seems not at all unreasonable that excellent predictions would be yielded by the hypothesis that the billiard player made his shots *as if* he knew the formulas, could estimate accurately by eye the angles, etc., describing the location of the balls, could make lightning calculations from the formulas, and could then make the ball travel in the direction indicated by the formulas. It would in no way disprove or contradict the hypothesis, or weaken our confidence in it, if it should turn out that the billiard player had never studied any branch of mathematics and was utterly incapable of making the necessary calculations: unless he was capable in some way of reaching approximately the same result as that obtained from the formulas, he would not in fact be likely to be an expert billiard player.

The same considerations are relevant to our utility hypothesis. Whatever the psychological mechanism whereby individuals make choices, these choices appear to display some consistency, which can apparently be described by our utility hypothesis. This hypothesis enables predictions to be made about phenomena on which there is not yet reliable evidence. The hypothesis cannot be declared invalid for a particular class of behavior until a prediction about that class proves false. No other test of its validity is decisive.

The last paragraph of this passage is admirable for its emphasis on prediction of choice behavior in counterfactual settings. However, I find it much less agreeable when Friedman and Savage propose that their "utility hypothesis" (that is, expected utility maximization and rational expectations) should be used to predict behavior until observation of behavior is able to refute the hypothesis. Many models of behavior may be consistent with available choice data. The assumption of rational expectations is often suspect.

Why then do Friedman and Savage put forward one hypothesis, to the exclusion of all others? The reader may recall Friedman's own answer to this question, which I quoted in Chapter 1 and repeat here (Friedman 1953, 10):

> The choice among alternative hypotheses equally consistent with the available evidence must to some extent be arbitrary, though there is general agreement that relevant considerations are suggested by the criteria "simplicity" and "fruitfulness," themselves notions that defy completely objective specification.

I found this answer unsatisfactory earlier and reiterate here. I see no reason why a scientist should choose to make predictions under a single hypothesis, dismissing others that are plausible and consistent with the available evidence. Doing so gives an impression of predictive power that one does not really have.

Bounded Rationality

Although many economists have found *as-if* rationality a compelling rationale for the assumptions they maintain, other researchers have, with equal fervor, dismissed the notion out of hand. Simon (1955, 101) put it this way in the article that spawned the modern literature in behavioral economics:

> Because of the psychological limits of the organism (particularly with respect to computational and predictive ability), actual human rationality-striving can at best be an extremely crude and simplified approximation to the kind of global rationality that is implied, for example, by game-theoretical models.

This notion has come to be called *bounded rationality.* Simon put forward this mission for research on behavior (p. 99):

> Broadly stated, the task is to replace the global rationality of economic man with a kind of rational behavior that is compatible with the access to information and the computational capacities that are actually possessed by organisms, including man, in the kinds of environments in which such organisms exist.

He went on to suggest that humans suffice with a coarse delineation between satisfactory and unsatisfactory outcomes, an idea that has come to be called *satisficing.*

A striking aspect of Simon's article is that it neither reports nor cites empirical evidence on actual human decision processes, save for a footnote briefly describing a personal observation. Instead, Simon relies on his own interpretation of "common experience (p. 100):

> Lacking the kinds of empirical knowledge of the decisional processes that will be required for a definitive theory, the hard facts of the actual world can, at the present stage, enter the theory only in a relatively unsystematic and unrigorous way. But none of us is completely innocent of acquaintance with the gross characteristics of human choice, or of the broad features of the environment in which this choice takes place. I shall feel free to call on this common experience as a source of the hypotheses needed for the theory about the nature of man and his world.

Thus, although the articles of Simon and Friedman-Savage put forward sharply contrasting hypotheses about human behavior, both articles were essentially speculative.

Biases and Heuristics

In the absence of empirical evidence, researchers with worldviews as divergent as Simon and Friedman-Savage might argue forever without any prospect for convergence. After a slow beginning in the 1950s and 1960s, a substantial body of empirical research has accumulated since the 1970s. The dominant mode of research has been that of experimental psychology, which has been adopted as well by experimental economics.

Research on choice behavior in experimental psychology usually means the design and performance of experiments that give subjects specified information and require them to choose among specified actions. The subjects typically are a convenience sample of persons, often students at some college, rather than a random sample drawn from a population of policy interest. The proximate objective of the research usually is to test or demonstrate hypotheses about human perception, cognition, and decision processes. Prediction of choice behavior in new settings hardly ever forms part of the explicit agenda, although it may be an implicit reason for performing a study.

The research program of Daniel Kahneman and Amos Tversky has been particularly influential, both within and beyond the discipline of psychology. Tversky and Kahneman (1974) reported experiments on subjective assessments of probability before and after the provision of sample data. They observed some systematic inconsistencies with the theoretically correct use of Bayes Theorem, a basic principle of probability theory, to integrate new data with prior beliefs. They called these inconsistencies *biases.* The authors concluded that persons tend to use certain heuristics to process sample data rather than perform the algebra needed to apply Bayes Theorem. They wrote (p. 1124): "In general, these heuristics are quite useful, but sometimes they lead to severe and systematic errors." This statement is much in the spirit of Simon's bounded rationality.

Kahneman and Tversky (1979) reported experiments on decision making that showed some systematic inconsistencies with the predictions of expected utility theory. They interpreted the observed choice behavior as demonstrating that persons evaluate actions in terms of gains and losses relative to a predetermined reference point, rather than in terms of absolute outcomes as in expected utility theory. They also interpreted observed behavior as demonstrating that persons evaluate gains and losses asymmetrically. They went on to embody these and other behavioral features in a model that they called *prospect theory.* As presented in the 1979 article, prospect theory assumes that decision makers solve well-defined maximization problems cast in terms of gains and losses. Thus, it is not a wholesale rejection of economic thinking but rather a revision to expected utility theory to render what the authors believed to be a more accurate description of behavior.

Tversky and Kahneman (1981, 1986) reported further experiments on decision making that explore how choice behavior depends on the *framing* of the decision problem—that is, on the language that the researcher uses to describe the outcomes resulting from alternative actions. These experiments had striking results. I quote here the statement and interpretation of the first experiment reported in the former article, which has drawn particular attention (Tversky and Kahneman, 1981, 453). In what follows, Problem 1 and Problem 2 are two alternative framings of the decision problem. The sample sizes and fractions of subjects making each choice are in brackets.

Problem 1 [$N = 152$]:
    Imagine that the U.S. is preparing for the outbreak of an unusual Asian disease, which is expected to kill 600 people. Two alternative

programs to combat the disease have been proposed. Assume that the exact scientific estimate of the consequences of the programs are as follows:

If Program A is adopted, 200 people will be saved. [72 percent]

If Program B is adopted, there is ⅓ probability that 600 people will be saved, and ⅔ probability that no people will be saved. [28 percent]

Which of the two programs would you favor?

The majority choice in this problem is risk averse: the prospect of certainly saving 200 lives is more attractive than a risky prospect of equal expected value, that is, a one-in-three chance of saving 600 lives.

A second group of respondents was given the cover story of problem 1 with a different formulation of the alternative programs, as follows:

Problem 2 [*N* = 155]:

    If Program C is adopted 400 people will die. [22 percent]

    If Program D is adopted there is ⅓ probability that nobody will die, and ⅔ probability that 600 people will die. [78 percent]

    Which of the two programs would you favor?

    The majority choice in problem 2 is risk taking: the certain death of 400 people is less acceptable than the two-in-three chance that 600 will die. The preferences in problems 1 and 2 illustrate a common pattern: choices involving gains are often risk averse and choices involving losses are often risk taking. However, it is easy to see that the two problems are effectively identical. The only difference between them is that the outcomes are described in problem 1 by the number of lives saved and in problem 2 by the number of lives lost.

Tversky and Kahneman drew strong inferences from this and similar findings in other framing experiments. They concluded not only that expected utility theory is unrealistic but that human behavior is inconsistent with the basic *invariance* tenet of rational choice, this being that "different representations of the same choice problem should yield the same preferences" (Tversky and Kahneman, 1986, S253). Dismissing the basic economic idea that persons have stable preferences, they ultimately declared that "the normative and the descriptive analyses of choice should be viewed as separate enterprises" (p. S275). This statement abandoned the Simon view of human behavior as a boundedly rational approximation to a rational ideal. It suggested that psychology should go its own way as a descriptive science of human behavior, no longer concerned with the way that economists conceptualize and study choice behavior.

Widespread Irrationality or Occasional Cognitive Illusions?

The specific experimental findings reported by Kahneman and Tversky during the course of their research program are not in question. The experiments described above have been replicated often, with broadly similar results. However, acceptance of the findings does not imply that one should accept the inferences that Kahneman and Tversky drew from them. Their conclusions that the experiments reveal general features of human behavior are huge extrapolations.

Consider the Asian-disease framing experiment cited above. In the passage describing the experiment, Tversky and Kahneman gave their prospect-theory interpretation of the findings; that is, persons are risk averse when considering gains and risk taking when considering losses. They did not entertain other interpretations that are consistent with the findings. One such is that the subject pool contains many persons who are risk neutral; that is, persons who evaluate a choice alternative by its expected outcome.

All of the treatment programs posed in the experiment yield the same expected outcome, namely that 200 people will live and 400 will die. Thus, a risk-neutral person is indifferent among the programs. If the choice behavior of such a person is affected by the framing of Problems 1 and 2, this is not evidence for prospect theory and does not imply failure of the invariance tenet of rationality.

While some psychologists have joined Kahneman and Tversky in extrapolating from particular laboratory experiments to general human behavior, others have not. Review articles by Shanteau (1989), Stanovich and West (2000), and Kühberger (2002) describe the variation in perspective across psychologists. Lopes (1991) deconstructs the rhetoric that Kahneman and Tversky used in reporting their research.

An important reason why it is difficult to assess the external validity of the Kahneman-Tversky experiments is that these experiments reflected a purposeful search for choice tasks in which errors in judgment and decision making are prominent. Kahneman and Tversky (1982, 123) argued that purposeful search for errors is a useful methodological approach:

Much of the recent literature on judgment and inductive reasoning has been concerned with errors, biases and fallacies in a variety of mental tasks. . . . The emphasis on the study of errors is characteristic of research in human judgment, but is not unique to this domain: we use illusions to understand the principles of normal perception and we learn about memory by studying forgetting.

They later elaborated (p. 124):

There are three related reasons for the focus on systematic errors and inferential biases in the study of reasoning. First, they expose some of our intellectual limitations and suggest ways of improving the quality of our thinking. Second, errors and biases often reveal the psychological processes and the heuristic procedures that govern judgment and inference. Third, mistakes and fallacies help the mapping of human intuitions by indicating which principles of statistics or logic are non-intuitive or counter-intuitive.

This methodological approach may have scientific merit. However, the Kahneman-Tversky emphasis on the study of errors and biases creates a severe inferential problem for a reader of their published research. One learns the findings of the experiments that they report, which invariably show that errors and biases are commonplace. However, one learns nothing about the findings that would occur in experiments that they either do not report or did not perform.

Consider again the Asian-disease framing experiment. How would subjects behave if the stated numbers of deaths and lives saved were changed, so that a risk-neutral person would not be indifferent between treatment programs (A, B, C, D)? Would the strong framing effect persist, or would it diminish as the welfare consequence of the decision becomes larger?

One could, of course, perform and report experiments that answer these questions. The Kahneman and Tversky articles on framing did not indicate whether such experiments were performed and, if so, what the findings were. Thus, one cannot know whether the published findings demonstrate that humans are prone to widespread irrationality or only occasional cognitive illusions.

The Common Thread Is Certitude

To wrap up, an enormous scientific distance separates the Friedman-Savage contention that *as-if* rationality well approximates human behavior from the Kahneman-Tversky contention that persons lack stable preferences. The common thread in the rhetoric of both sets of authors is expression of certitude in their opposing perspectives. Dueling certitudes continues today to characterize much discussion of human behavior, which often simplistically debates whether humans are or are not rational. The more nuanced perspective of Simon draws some attention, but less than I think it warrants.

II

POLICY DECISIONS

4

⇒◆⇐

Planning with Partial Knowledge

PART I explained the immense difficulty of predicting policy outcomes. I observed that the point predictions produced by analysts are achieved by imposing strong assumptions that rarely have foundation. Analysis with more credible assumptions typically yields interval rather than point predictions.

Part II considers how policy making may reasonably cope with this difficulty. Chapter 4 and part of Chapter 5 use elementary ideas of decision theory to study policy choice by a *planner*—an actual or idealized solitary decision maker who acts on behalf of society. Part of Chapter 5 and Chapter 6 will discuss policy choice when a group with heterogeneous objectives and beliefs collectively make decisions.

Why study a planner, when policy in democracies emerges from the interaction of many persons and institutions? Policy choice in an uncertain world is subtle even when a society agrees on what it wants and what it believes. I want to drive home the point that, even in such a cohesive society, there is no optimal decision, at most various reasonable ones. A planner personifies a cohesive society that forthrightly acknowledges and copes with uncertainty.

This chapter studies a relatively simple setting in which a planner makes an isolated decision with predetermined partial knowledge of policy outcomes. Thus, there is no opportunity to obtain new data that might reduce the extent of uncertainty. Chapter 5 will consider sequential choice settings, which bring opportunities for learning.

4.1. Treating X-Pox

I begin with a simple illustration drawn from Manski (2007a, chap. 11). The illustration describes a dire but hopefully hypothetical scenario.

Suppose that a new disease called x-pox is sweeping a community. It is impossible to avoid infection. If untreated, infected persons always die. Thus, the entire population will die in the absence of effective treatment.

Medical researchers propose two treatments, say *A* and *B*. The researchers know that one treatment is effective, but they do not know which one. They know that administering both treatments in combination is fatal. Thus, a person will survive if and only if she is administered the effective treatment alone. There is no time to experiment to learn which treatment is effective. Everyone must be treated right away.

A public health agency must decide how to treat the community. The agency wants to maximize the survival rate of the population. It can select one treatment and administer it to everyone. Then the entire population will either live or die. Or it can give one treatment to some fraction of the community and the other treatment to the remaining fraction. Then the survival rate will be one of the two chosen fractions. If half the population receives each treatment, the survival rate is certain to be 50 percent.

What should the agency do? It could give everyone the same treatment and hope to make the right choice, recognizing the possibility that the outcome may be calamitous. Or it could give half the population each treatment, ensuring that half the community lives and half dies. One can reasonably argue for either alternative. Indeed, the principles of decision theory developed in the next several sections can be used to motivate either course of action.

4.2. Elements of Decision Theory

Decision theory aims to prescribe how a rational decision maker should behave or, less ambitiously, contemplates how one might reasonably behave. I will use elementary principles of decision theory to examine how a planner might choose policy. This chapter introduces the principles and illustrates their application. Chapter 5 develops further applications.

Suppose that a decision maker—perhaps a firm, an individual, or a planner—must choose an action from a set of feasible alternatives. Each action will yield an outcome of some sort. The decision maker places values on outcomes, commonly called *utility* in research on private decisions and *welfare* in studies of planning. I will use the latter term here.

If the decision maker knows the welfare that each action will yield, he should choose one that yields the highest welfare. How might he reasonably behave if he does not know the outcomes that will occur? Decision theory addresses this question.

States of Nature

To formalize the idea of partial knowledge, suppose that outcomes are determined by the chosen action and by some feature of the environment. Decision theorists call the relevant feature of the environment the *state of nature*. Going further, they suppose that the decision maker is able to list all the states of nature that he believes could possibly occur. This list, called the *state space*, formally expresses partial knowledge. For example, the state space in the x-pox illustration contained two states of nature. Treatment *A* was effective in one state and *B* was effective in the other.

Prediction with certitude occurs if the state space contains just one element. Then the decision maker knows for sure the outcome of each action. Interval prediction of policy outcomes occurs if the state space contains multiple elements. The larger the state space, the less the decision maker knows about the consequences of each action.

The fundamental difficulty of decision making is clear even in a simple setting with two feasible actions and two states of nature. Suppose that one action yields higher welfare in one state of nature, but the other action yields higher welfare in the other state. Then the decision maker does not know which action is better.

Decision theory does not explain how a decision maker forms the state space. Presumably, he uses available data and assumptions to determine the environments that he thinks might possibly occur. Whatever the state space may be, it is meant to expresses the knowledge that the decision maker finds credible to assert. It does not express incredible certitude.

Recall Rumsfeld's distinction between "known unknowns" and "unknown unknowns" cited at the beginning of this book. Decision theory formalizes uncertainty as the former rather than the latter. When we say that a decision maker lists all possible states of nature and determines the welfare that would result when any action is combined with any state, we are saying that he faces known unknowns. If there were unknown unknowns, he would not be able to list all possible states.

Rumsfeld declared "it is the latter category that tend to be the difficult ones" for policy choice. He was right to call attention to the special difficulty posed by unknown unknowns. However, it is sanguine to downplay the known unknowns. They are difficult enough.

The Welfare Function

Next let us formalize the welfare that results from choosing an action. If a decision maker chooses an action labeled C, and a state of nature labeled s occurs, the result is a welfare value labeled $W(C, s)$. To summarize, action C and state of nature s yield welfare $W(C, s)$. Whereas the state space expresses the knowledge that a decision maker possesses, the welfare function expresses his preferences. The higher the welfare value, the better off is the decision maker. Decision theory is silent on the nature of the welfare function. Preferences are whatever they may be.

The field of welfare economics, which applies decision theory to policy choice, manifests two perspectives on the welfare function. In some studies, the planner is considered to be a decision maker who uses his own preferences to make decisions. The planner may be called a *dictator* or *paternalistic*.

In other studies, the planner personifies a cohesive society. When this perspective is used, economists introspect on what such a society might want to achieve and formalize social preferences as a welfare function. A prominent tradition has been to suppose that social preferences take the form of a *utilitarian* welfare function, which aggregates the private preferences of members of the population. A common expression of utilitarianism supposes that the welfare produced by a policy is a weighted average of the individual utilities generated by the policy.

In principle, researchers interpreting the planner as a dictator should consult this decision maker to learn his social preferences. Those operating in the utilitarian tradition should consult the members of the population to learn their private preferences. In practice, researchers performing planning studies typically do neither. Rather, they make assumptions about the social preferences of a dictator or the private preferences of population members. They then study policy choice using the welfare function that they themselves invent.

Citizens concerned with policy choice need to be aware that the policy choices recommended in planning studies depend fundamentally on the welfare functions that researchers use. I wrote at the beginning of Chapter 2 that, in an ideal world, persons who are not expert in research methodology would be able to trust the conclusions of policy analysis, without concern about the process used to produce them. I cautioned, however, that consumers of policy analysis cannot safely trust the experts and, hence, need to comprehend at least the main features of research methodology.

I was writing then about the predictions of policy outcomes, particularly the tendency of analysts to assert certitude. The same caution applies to interpretation of the findings of planning studies. When an analyst concludes that some policy choice is optimal, this conclusion necessarily depends on the welfare function used. I will use income tax policy to illustrate.

Welfare Functions in Studies of Optimal Income Taxation

A familiar exercise in normative public economics poses a utilitarian social welfare function and ranks income tax policies by the welfare they achieve. The starting point is the presumption that individuals value their own income and leisure, as well as government production of public goods. Examples of public goods range from national defense and local policing to infrastructure for transportation, communications, and economic activity. The policy choice problem is to set an income tax schedule and to decide how to use the resulting tax revenue. One possible use of tax revenue is to redistribute income across persons. Another is to produce public goods. An optimal policy chooses the tax schedule and use of tax revenues to maximize utilitarian social welfare. The optimal policy necessarily depends on individual preferences for income, leisure, and public goods. It also depends on how the planner aggregates the preferences of the population.

The Mirrlees Study

I will describe the welfare function used by James Mirrlees in his pioneering study of optimal income taxation (Mirrlees 1971). Mirrlees adopted the utilitarian perspective, writing (p. 176): "welfare is separable in terms of the different individuals of the economy, and symmetric—-i.e. it can be expressed as the sum of the utilities of individuals when the individual utility function (the same for all) is suitably chosen." Beyond its expression of utilitarianism, this sentence calls attention to another important assumption of the Mirrlees planning study. That is, he supposed that all members of the population share the same private preferences.

Mirrlees restricted the function of government to redistribution of income from some members of the population to others. Redistribution has long been a concern of utilitarian welfare economics. However, public economics also stresses the governmental function of production of public goods. The Mirrlees model supposed that utility is a function of private income and leisure alone. There are no public goods and, hence, no need for the government to have tax revenue to produce them.

Mirrlees used the textbook model of labor supply described in Section 3.1 to predict the tax revenue produced by a policy and to evaluate the welfare achieved by use of tax revenue to redistribute income. To perform his analysis, Mirrlees had to specify the utility function that he assumed to be common to all members of the population. He was a theorist, not an empirical analyst who might seek to learn the nature of private preferences from analysis of labor supply data. For reasons of analytical tractability rather than empirical realism, he assumed that the utility function had certain properties. He then derived the optimal tax policy.

In calling attention to the particular form of welfare function that Mirrlees used, I do not intend to criticize his work, which I admire. When opening up a new area of study, a researcher should have some license to make simplifying assumptions for the sake of analytical tractability. Mirrlees was careful to make his assumptions explicit, and he did not assert incredible certitude. Indeed, the concluding section of his article begins as follows (p. 207):

> The examples discussed confirm, as one would expect, that the shape of the optimum earned-income tax schedule is rather sensitive to the distribution of skills within the population, and to the income-leisure preferences postulated. Neither is easy to estimate for real economies. The simple consumption-leisure utility function is a heroic abstraction from a much more complicated situation, so that it is quite hard to guess what a satisfactory method of estimating it would be.

Thus, Mirrlees took care to point out that conclusions about optimal tax policy are sensitive to the assumptions made.

4.3. Decision Criteria

Elimination of Dominated Actions

How might a decision maker with partial knowledge choose an action? Decision theory gives a simple partial answer, but no complete answer.

Contemplating some action D, a decision maker might find that there exists another feasible action, say C, that yields at least as high welfare in every state of nature and higher welfare in some states. Then action D is said to be *dominated* by C.

Decision theory prescribes that one should not choose a dominated action. This is common sense. Uncertainty is inconsequential when evaluating a dominated action. Even though one does not know the true state of nature, one knows that an alternative to a dominated action surely performs at least as well and may perform better.

Dominance is a simple idea, but a subtle one. A common misconception is that an action is undominated only if it is optimal in some state of nature. In fact, an action may be undominated even if it is suboptimal in every possible state.

The x-pox scenario illustrates this well. Consider the policy in which the planner gives half the population each treatment. There is no state of nature in which this policy is optimal. Treatment A is better in one state and B is better in the other. Yet giving half the population each treatment is undominated. There exists no alternative that yields higher welfare in both states of nature.

Weighting States and the Expected Welfare Criterion

The rationale for elimination of dominated actions is self-evident. In contrast, choice among undominated actions is fundamentally problematic. Suppose that C and D are two undominated actions, with C yielding higher welfare in some states of nature and D in others. Then the normative question "How should the decision maker choose between C and D?" has no unambiguously correct answer.

In the absence of one correct way to choose among undominated actions, decision theorists have proposed various decision criteria and studied their properties. Many decision theorists recommend that one weight the possible states of nature and evaluate an action by the resulting weighted average welfare. This is called the *expected utility* or *expected welfare* of an action. The recommendation is to choose an action that yields the largest expected welfare. Chapter 3 discussed maximization of expected utility as a behavioral assumption used by economists to interpret actual decision making. Here we consider it as a normative prescription for decision making.

A central issue is how to weight the possible states of nature. Decision theorists suggest that the weight assigned to a state should express the strength of the decision maker's belief that this state will occur. The weight is the subjective probability that the decision maker places on the state. The body of research studying the behavior of someone who weights states of nature in this way and chooses an action yielding the largest expected welfare is often called *Bayesian decision theory*. This name honors the eighteenth-century British mathematician Thomas Bayes, previously mentioned in Chapter 3 in connection with Bayes Theorem.

The selected weights affect decision making. At the extreme, a decision maker might concentrate all weight on a single state of nature. This is tantamount to expression of certitude. When all weight is placed on one state, an action maximizes expected welfare if it is optimal in this state, disregarding all others.

Criteria for Decision Making under Ambiguity

Weighting states of nature and maximization of expected welfare is reasonable when a decision maker has a credible basis for placing a subjective probability distribution on unknown features of the decision environment. However, a decision maker may feel that he lacks a basis for weighting states according to strength of belief. A subjective distribution is a form of knowledge, and a decision maker may not feel able to assert one.

In these circumstances, the decision maker is said to face a problem of choice under *ambiguity*. Use of the term *ambiguity* to describe the absence of a subjective distribution originated in Ellsberg (1961). The concept was discussed as early as Keynes (1921) and Knight (1921). Some authors refer to ambiguity as *Knightian uncertainty*.

Maximin

How might a decision maker reasonably behave in a setting of ambiguity? One possibility is to evaluate an action by the worst welfare that it may yield and choose an action that yields the least-bad worst welfare. Someone who chooses in this manner is said to apply the *maximin* criterion, this being an abbreviation for "maximization of minimum" welfare.

Minimax Regret

The maximin criterion offers a conservative approach to choice under ambiguity, considering only the worst outcome that an action may yield. Other criteria that do not require weighting states of nature consider both best and worst outcomes. A prominent one is the minimax-regret criterion.

The *Oxford English Dictionary* gives several definitions for the word *regret*. The decision-theoretic concept of regret is closest to this definition: "Sorrow or distress at a loss or deprivation." In decision theory, the regret of an action in a particular state of nature is the loss in welfare that would occur if one were to choose this action rather than the one that is best in this state of nature. Suppose, for example, that action C maximizes welfare in state s, but one were to choose action D instead. Then the regret from choosing D in this state is the welfare difference $W(C, s) - W(D, s)$.

A decision maker who knows the true state of nature can choose the action that is best in this state. Then his regret equals zero. Thus, maximizing welfare is the same as minimizing regret.

The actual decision problem requires choice of an action without knowing the true state. In this context, the decision maker can evaluate an action by the maximum regret that it may yield across all possible states of nature. He can then choose an action that minimizes the value of maximum regret. Someone who chooses in this manner is said to use the *mimimax-regret* criterion, this being an abbreviation for "minimization of maximum" regret.

Using Different Criteria to Treat X-Pox

It is revealing to juxtapose the three decision criteria—expected welfare, maximin, and minimax regret—in particular decision settings. Consider the x-pox scenario. The feasible actions are treatment allocations, assigning a fraction of the population to each treatment. The fraction assigned to treatment A can take any value from zero to one, the remainder being assigned to B. There are two states of nature, say s and t. In state s, treatment A is effective and B is not. In state t, B is effective and A is not.

Let welfare be measured by the survival rate of the population. If the planner assigns a fraction d of the population to treatment B and the remaining $1-d$ to treatment A, the survival rate is d in state t and is $1-d$ in state s.

With this knowledge and welfare function, all treatment allocations are undominated. Compare any two fractions c and d, with c larger than d. Assigning fraction c of the population to treatment B outperforms assigning d in state t, but it underperforms d in state s.

Now consider a planner who applies each of the three decision criteria. Appendix A shows that a planner who places subjective probabilities on the two states of nature and evaluates a treatment allocation by its expected welfare would assign everyone to the treatment with the higher subjective probability of being effective. In contrast, the maximin and the minimax-regret criteria both prescribe that the planner should assign half the population to each treatment. *Ex post,* a planner who maximizes the expected survival rate finds that either everyone lives or everyone dies. One who maximizes the minimum survival rate or minimizes maximum regret achieves a survival rate of ½ with certitude.

Although the maximin and minimax-regret criteria deliver the same treatment allocation in this illustration, the two criteria are not the same in general. They more typically yield different choices. To see this, let us amend the description of the x-pox problem by adding a third state of nature, say u, in which neither treatment is effective. It can be shown that adding this third state does not affect the choices made by a planner who maximizes expected welfare or minimizes maximum regret. However, all treatment allocations now solve the maximin problem. The reason is that there now exists a possible state of nature in which everyone dies, regardless of treatment.

4.4. Search Profiling with Partial Knowledge of Deterrence

The x-pox scenario is pedagogically useful but intentionally simplistic. I summarize here a more realistic study of planning with partial knowledge, considering an aspect of law enforcement that has been the subject of considerable debate (Manski 2006). This is the choice of a *profiling* policy wherein decisions to search for evidence of crime may vary with observable attributes of the persons at risk of being searched.

Policies that make search rates vary with personal attributes are variously defended as essential to effective law enforcement and denounced as unfair to classes of persons subjected to relatively high search rates. Variation of search rates by race has been particularly controversial; see, for example, Knowles, Persico, and Todd (2001), Persico (2002), and Dominitz (2003). Whereas much research on profiling has sought to define and detect racial discrimination, I studied how a planner with a utilitarian welfare function might reasonably choose a profiling policy.

To begin, I posed a planning problem whose objective is to minimize the social cost of crime and search. (Maximizing welfare is equivalent to minimizing social cost.) I supposed that search is costly per se, and search that reveals a crime entails costs for punishment of offenders. Search is beneficial to the extent that it deters or prevents crime. Deterrence is expressed through the *offense function*, which describes how the offense rate of persons with given attributes varies with the search rate applied to these persons. Prevention occurs when search prevents an offense from causing social harm.

I first derived the optimal profiling policy when the planner knows the offense function of each attribute group. An interesting finding was that it may be optimal to search a less crime-prone group and not to search a more crime-prone group if members of the former group can be deterred and those in the latter group cannot.

I then examined the planning problem when the planner has only partial knowledge of the offense function and hence is unable to determine what policy is optimal. Prediction of deterrence is difficult. With this in mind, I focused on an informational setting that may sometimes be realistic.

I supposed that the planner observes the offense rates of a study population whose attribute-specific search rates have previously been chosen. He finds it credible to assume that the study population and the population of interest have the same offense function. He also finds it credible to assume that search deters crime. That is, in each attribute group, the offense rate decreases as the search rate increases. However, I supposed that the planner does not know the magnitude of the deterrent effect of search, which may differ by group.

In this setting, I first showed how the planner can eliminate dominated search rates—that is, search rates that are inferior whatever the actual offense function may be. Broadly speaking, low (high) search rates are dominated when the cost of search is low (high). The technical analysis makes this precise. I then showed how the planner can use the maximin or minimax-regret criterion to choose an undominated search rate. The two criteria yield different policies.

Although detection of discrimination was not my direct concern, the analysis has implications for that inferential problem. The models studied in Knowles, Persico, and Todd (2001) and in Persico (2002) imply that, in the absence of discrimination, optimal profiling must equalize the offense rates of persons with different attributes, provided that such persons are searched at all. The model in Manski (2006) differs from theirs, and it does not produce their conclusion.

Perhaps the most important difference is in the welfare function assumed for the agency that makes profiling policy. Persico and his collaborators assumed that police on the street aim to maximize the success rate of search in detecting crime minus the cost of performing searches. I assumed that a planner wants to minimize a social cost function with three components: (a) the harm caused by completed offenses, (b) the cost of punishing offenders who are apprehended, and (c) the cost of performing searches. Whereas the Persico et al. welfare function does not value deterrence, the one I used does. This difference in welfare functions turns out to be highly consequential for policy choice.

4.5. Vaccination with Partial Knowledge of Effectiveness

I describe here another study of planning with partial knowledge whose subject matter is distant from police search but whose formal structure is similar. Manski (2010) studied choice of vaccination policy by a planner who has partial knowledge of the effectiveness of the vaccine in preventing illness. I first provide some background and then summarize the analysis.

Background

The problem of choosing a vaccination policy for a population susceptible to infectious disease has drawn considerable attention from epidemiologists, and some from economists as well. A common research exercise uses an epidemiological model to forecast the illness outcomes that would occur with alternative policies. The researcher then specifies a welfare function and determines the optimal policy under the assumption that the epidemiological model is accurate.

To give one among many recent examples, Patel, Longini, and Halloran (2005) considered the optimal targeting of a limited supply of influenza vaccine to minimize the number of illnesses or deaths in a population. The discussion section of the article summarized a key finding (p. 210):

> We have shown that the optimal vaccine distributions are highly effective, especially when compared to random mass vaccination. Implementation of the optimal vaccine distribution for Asian-like pandemic influenza was found to be 84% more effective than random vaccination when there was only enough vaccine for 30% of the entire vaccination and the objective was to minimize illness. This optimal vaccination strategy involved concentrating vaccine in children, with the leftover vaccine going to middle aged adults. In this situation, given a population of 280 million people, we would be able to prevent 31 million illnesses following the optimal vaccination strategy rather than random mass vaccination.

Observe that the authors expressed their finding with certitude. Vaccination researchers have largely not studied planning with partial knowledge. They occasionally acknowledge uncertainty by performing sensitivity analyses in which they determine optimal policy under alternative assumptions. However, sensitivity analysis does not provide a prescription for choice with partial knowledge.

Internal and External Effectiveness

There are two reasons why a health planner may have only partial knowledge of the effect of vaccination on illness. He may only partially know the *internal effectiveness* of vaccination in generating an immune response that prevents a vaccinated person from becoming ill or infectious. And he may only partially know the *external effectiveness* of vaccination in preventing transmission of disease to members of the population who are unvaccinated or unsuccessfully vaccinated. Internal effectiveness is the only concern if response to vaccination is individualistic. External effectiveness measures the extent to which vaccination yields social interactions.

Learning about external effectiveness is much more difficult than learning about internal effectiveness. A standard RCT can reveal the internal effectiveness of vaccination. One may randomly draw a treatment group from the population, vaccinate them, and observe the fraction who experience an immune reaction following vaccination. An RCT does not reveal the external effect of vaccination on the unvaccinated. Suppose that a trial vaccinates some fraction of the population, say 20 percent. Then observation of the subsequent illness rate only reveals the external effectiveness of vaccinating 20 percent of the population. The illness outcomes with all other vaccination rates are counterfactual.

If persons interact only within local areas, one might learn about external effectiveness by performing multiple independent trials in different locales, varying the vaccination rate across trials. However, this is not feasible if persons interact globally. Then the population comprises a single reference group, so it is impossible to perform multiple trials.

Lacking evidence from RCTs, vaccination researchers have invested heavily in the development of mathematical models of disease transmission. Some models embody impressive efforts to formally describe how individual behavior, social interactions, and biological processes may combine to spread disease within a population. However, authors typically provide little information that would enable one to assess the accuracy of their behavioral, social, and biological assumptions. Hence, I think it prudent to view their predictions of policy outcomes more as computational experiments than as accurate forecasts.

The Planning Problem

I posed a planning problem in which a planner must choose the vaccination rate for a large population of observationally identical persons. Having the members of the population be observationally identical does not presume that persons respond identically to treatment. It only means that the planner does not observe personal attributes that would enable him to vary treatment systematically across the population.

I supposed that the planner wants to maximize a welfare function with two components. One measures the social harm caused by illness, and the other measures the social cost of vaccinating persons. I took the social harm of illness to be proportional to the fraction of the population who become ill and the cost of vaccination to be proportional to the fraction of the population who are vaccinated. This welfare function expresses the core tension of vaccination policy: a higher vaccination rate yields the benefit of a lower rate of illness but incurs a larger cost of vaccinating persons.

Similar welfare functions have been assumed in some past research on optimal vaccination, such as Brito, Sheshinski, and Intriligator (1991). However, it has been more common to assume that the objective is to keep the transmission rate of disease below the threshold at which an epidemic occurs. See, for example, Ball and Lynne (2002) or Hill and Longini (2003). The latter authors ask (p. 86): "What minimal fraction of each age group should be vaccinated to eliminate the possibility of an influenza epidemic in the whole population?"

The objective of preventing onset of an epidemic may differ from maximization of social welfare. In epidemiology, an epidemic is formally defined to occur when the infected fraction of the population increases with time. In contrast, the welfare function posed in my work abstracts from the time path of illness and considers the prevalence of illness in the population.

Partial Knowledge of External Effectiveness

The optimal vaccination rate depends on the internal and external effectiveness of vaccination. I supposed that the planner completely knows internal effectiveness, perhaps from performance of an RCT. He uses empirical evidence and assumptions to draw partial conclusions about external effectiveness.

The evidence derives from observation of the vaccination and illness rates of a study population. I supposed that the planner finds it credible to assume that external effectiveness is the same in the study population and the treatment population. He also finds it credible to assume that the illness rate of unvaccinated persons decreases as the vaccination rate increases. I supposed that the planner has no other knowledge. In particular, he knows nothing about the degree to which infection decreases as the vaccination rate rises.

This informational setting is analogous to the one I described in the last section, when considering choice of a rate of police search when the planner has partial knowledge of the deterrent effect of search. The assumptions that search deters crime and that vaccination prevents transmission of disease are two examples of *monotone treatment response*, an often credible and useful assumption asserting that the prevalence of a bad outcome falls monotonically as the magnitude of a beneficial treatment rises (Manski 1997b).

Choosing a Vaccination Rate

It might be thought that the monotonicity assumption is too weak to yield interesting implications for treatment choice. However, it has considerable power in the vaccination setting, as it did with police search. It implies that small (large) vaccination rates are dominated when the cost of vaccinating persons is sufficiently small (large) relative to the harm due to illness.

With dominated vaccination rates eliminated from consideration, the planner must still choose among the undominated rates. I derived the maximin and minimax-regret rates. The planner might choose to vaccinate no one, the entire population, or some fraction of the population. The specific findings depend jointly on the data obtained from the study population, the relative costs of illness and vaccination, and the decision criterion used.

The findings of this study may be used to form vaccination policy when a public health agency has the authority to mandate treatment, observes a study population, and is reluctant to assume more about external effectiveness than its monotonicity in the vaccination rate. Of course the findings are not universally applicable. They necessarily depend on my specification of the feasible policy choices, the welfare function, and the knowledge of treatment response possessed by the planner. What is universally applicable is the general approach: specify the planning problem, eliminate dominated policies, and then use some decision criterion to choose an undominated policy.

4.6. Rational and Reasonable Decision Making

I wrote near the beginning of this chapter that decision theory prescribes how a rational decision maker should behave or, less ambitiously, contemplates how a decision maker might reasonably behave. There has long been a tension between these perspectives on the mission of decision theory. This tension has practical and intellectual importance. I will discuss it at some length to conclude the chapter.

One perspective asserts that decision theory should prescribe particular procedures to choose among undominated actions. Adherence to these procedures is said to constitute rational decision making. The other perspective studies and compares various decision criteria without asserting that one is preeminent. As shorthand, I will say that the two perspectives respectively concern rational and reasonable decision making.

I expressed the reasonableness perspective when I wrote that there is no unambiguously correct way to choose among undominated actions. I examined three prominent decision criteria, but I did not recommend a particular one. My aims were more modest, to show that choice among decision criteria is consequential and to illustrate how the decision made may depend on the criterion used. The x-pox example demonstrated this dramatically.

The reasonableness perspective was expressed by Abraham Wald, a pioneer of statistical decision theory who studied the maximin criterion in depth. Wald did not contend that this criterion is optimal, only that it is reasonable. Semantically, Wald viewed the decision maker as wanting to minimize a loss function rather than maximize a welfare function. Hence, he used the term minimax rather than maximin. Early in his seminal book *Statistical Decision Functions,* Wald wrote (1950, 18): "a minimax solution seems, in general, to be a reasonable solution of the decision problem."

Perhaps the most influential proponent of the rationality perspective has been Leonard Savage, who also made landmark contributions to decision theory in the mid-twentieth century. In 1951, Savage argued strongly against the minimax criterion. Reviewing Wald (1950), he wrote (Savage 1951, 63): "Application of the minimax rule . . . is indeed ultra-pessimistic; no serious justification for it has ever been suggested."

Savage went on to propose the minimax-regret criterion, suggesting that it offers a more sensible approach to decision making. The minimax and minimax-regret criteria differ in how they measure loss. The former measures loss in absolute terms. The latter measures it relative to the best outcome achievable in a given state of nature. As a consequence, minimax regret is not "ultra-pessimistic."

Three years later, in his own seminal book *Foundations of Statistics,* Savage (1954) argued for the preeminence of the expected welfare criterion, asserting not only that a decision maker *might* use this criterion but that he *should* do so. He famously proved that adherence to certain *consistency axioms* on choice behavior is mathematically equivalent to placing a subjective probability distribution on the possible states of nature and maximizing expected welfare. He declared that adherence to his axioms constitutes rational behavior. He concluded that a decision maker should place a subjective distribution on his state space and should maximize expected welfare.

The Savage argument has been highly influential among applied economists, yet it was immediately controversial among decision theorists. A large and contentious literature has developed, expressing numerous perspectives. This book is not the right venue to summarize and review the literature. However, I will explain why I personally do not accept the Savage argument and do not think that the expected welfare criterion warrants a preeminent position among decision criteria. I begin by discussing the nature of Savage's argument for his consistency axioms.

The Savage Argument for Consistency

Savage worked in the branch of decision theory known as *axiomatic decision theory*. The staple formalism of axiomatic decision theory is a *representation theorem* that considers a collection of hypothetical choice scenarios and proposes axioms mandating consistency of behavior across scenarios. Such a theorem proves that adherence to the axioms is necessary and sufficient for behavior across scenarios to be representable as application of a particular decision criterion.

Consistency axioms are assertions that a person who would make particular choices in specified choice scenarios should, for the sake of consistency, make certain related choices in other scenarios. Perhaps the best known consistency axiom, and one of the easiest to contemplate, is transitivity.

Transitivity: Let C, D, and E be three actions. Consider three choice scenarios. In one setting, a decision maker must choose between C and D. In the second, he must choose between D and E. In the third, he must choose between C and E. Choice behavior is said to be *transitive* if a person who would choose C over D, and D over E, would also choose C over E.

Transitivity is simple to understand when action C dominates D and action D dominates E. The definition of dominance implies that C then dominates E. It follows logically that E should not be chosen over C.

The normative appeal of transitivity is more murky when the three actions are all undominated. Then logic does not dictate that someone who chooses C over D, and D over E, should choose C over E.

Nevertheless, Savage asserted that adherence to transitivity and several additional consistency axioms constitutes rational decision making with partial knowledge. In doing so, he recognized that logic per se does not require adherence to the axioms (p. 7):

> I am about to build up a highly idealized theory of the behavior of a "rational" person with respect to decisions. In doing so I will, of course, have to ask you to agree with me that such and such maxims of behavior are "rational." In so far as "rational" means logical, there is no live question; and, if I ask your leave there at all, it is only as a matter of form. But our person is going to have to make up his mind in situations

in which criteria beyond the ordinary ones of logic will be necessary. So, when certain maxims are presented for your consideration, you must ask yourself whether you try to behave in accordance with them, or, to put it differently, how you would react if you noticed yourself violating them.

Concerning the axiom of transitivity, he wrote this, referring to three actions as f, g, and h (p. 21):

> When it is explicitly brought to my attention that I have shown a preference for f as compared with g, for g as compared with h, and for h as compared with f, I feel uncomfortable in much the same way that I do when it is brought to my attention that some of my beliefs are logically contradictory. Whenever I examine such a triple of preferences on my own part, I find that it is not at all difficult to reverse one of them. In fact, I find that on contemplating the three alleged preferences side by side that at least one among them is not a preference at all, at any rate not any more.

In the first passage, Savage calls on his reader to introspect and to agree with him that his axioms have normative appeal as characteristics of rationality. In the second, he states that his own introspection reveals to him the desirability of transitivity.

Nothing in these passages argues that adhering to the Savage axioms produces substantively good decisions. Savage viewed consistency as a virtue per se. He wrote (p. 20): "It does not seem appropriate here to attempt an analysis of why and in what contexts we wish to be consistent; it is sufficient to allude to the fact that we often do wish to be so."

Axiomatic Rationality and Actualist Rationality

One may critique the Savage axioms from within axiomatic decision theory or from the outside. Internal critiques agree with Savage and with axiomatic decision theory more broadly that consistency of behavior across hypothetical choice scenarios is a virtue. The critique centers on the specific axioms proposed as having normative appeal. Appraisal of normative appeal in axiomatic decision theory rests on introspection, so there should be no expectation that consensus will emerge. Indeed, decision theorists exhibit considerable difference in opinion. A reader with sufficient mathematical background and interest in the continuing debate within axiomatic decision theory may want to read the monograph *Rational Decisions* of Binmore (2009), which catalogs and assesses a wide spectrum of consistency axioms.

External critiques take issue with the idea that adherence to consistency axioms is virtuous. In Manski (2011d), I argue that a person facing an actual decision problem is not concerned with the consistency of his behavior across hypothetical choice scenarios. He only wants to make a reasonable choice in the setting that he actually faces. Hence, normative decision theory should focus on what I call actualist rationality.

Actualist Rationality: Prescriptions for decision making should promote welfare maximization in the choice problem the agent actually faces.

The word *actualist* is seldom used in modern English, but an old definition captures the idea well.

Actualist: One who deals with or considers actually existing facts and conditions, rather than fancies or theories. (*Webster's Revised Unabridged Dictionary*, 1913 edition)

Actualist rationality differs from the rationality of axiomatic decision theory. In the language of philosophical ethics, actualist rationality is *consequentialist*—one values a prescription for decision making for its welfare consequences. The rationality of axiomatic theory is *deontological*—one values consistency of behavior across choice scenarios as a virtue per se.

From the perspective of actualist rationality, one need not join Savage in introspection regarding the normative appeal of his or other axioms. One rather rejects existing axiomatic decision theory as irrelevant to assessment of reasonable behavior with partial knowledge. Axiomatic theory would become relevant if researchers were to show that adherence to certain axioms promotes good decision making in practice. However, this has not been the objective of axiomatic theory to date.

Axiomatic and Actualist Perspectives on Subjective Probability

The difference between axiomatic and actualistic thinking is illustrated well by contrasting their conceptualizations of subjective probability distributions. The Savage consistency axioms make no reference to sub-jective probabilities. They arise only when Savage shows that adher-ence to the axioms is mathematically equivalent to placing a subjective probability distribution on the possible states of nature and maximiz-ing expected welfare.

From the actualist perspective, subjective probability is not a mathematical construct that is implicit in choice behavior. It is rather a psychological construct that persons use to make decisions. Arguing for the psychological realism of subjective probabilities, Tversky and Kahneman (1974, 1130) made plain the difference between the two perspectives:

> It should perhaps be noted that, while subjective probabilities can sometimes be inferred from preferences among bets, they are normally not formed in this fashion. A person bets on team A rather than on team B because he believes that team A is more likely to win; he does not infer this belief from his betting preferences. Thus, in reality, sub-jective probabilities determine preferences among bets and are not de-rived from them, as in the axiomatic theory of rational decision.

The statistical decision theorist James Berger has also contrasted the two perspectives (Berger 1985, 121), cautioning that "a Bayesian analysis may be 'rational' in the weak axiomatic sense, yet be terrible in a practical sense if an inappropriate prior distribution is used." Berg-er's comment expresses the actualist perspective that what matters is the performance of a decision criterion in practice. His use of the word "prior" refers to the subjective distribution that one holds before ob-serving some relevant empirical evidence.

Ellsberg on Ambiguity

Whereas the above passages presume that a decision maker places a subjective distribution on the possible states of nature, Daniel Ellsberg questioned this presumption. Ellsberg is widely known to the American public for his dissemination in 1971 of the Pentagon Papers. He is famous within decision theory for a seminal article (Ellsberg 1961) where he observed that thoughtful persons sometimes exhibit behavioral patterns that violate the Savage axioms in ways implying that they do not hold subjective distributions. Considering this behavior, he concluded his article (p. 669):

Are they foolish? It is not the object of this paper to judge that. I have been concerned rather to advance the testable propositions: (1) certain information states can be meaningfully identified as highly ambiguous; (2) in these states, many reasonable people tend to violate the Savage axioms with respect to certain choices; (3) their behavior is deliberate and not readily reversed upon reflection; (4) certain patterns of "violating" behavior can be distinguished and described in terms of a specified decision rule.

If these propositions should prove valid, the question of the optimality of this behavior would gain more interest. The mere fact that it conflicts with certain axioms of choice that at first glance appear reasonable does not seem to me to foreclose this question; empirical research, and even preliminary speculation, about the nature of actual or "successful" decision-making under uncertainty is still too young to give us confidence that these axioms are not abstracting away from vital considerations. It would seem incautious to rule peremptorily that the people in question should not allow their perception of ambiguity, their unease with their best estimates of probability, to influence their decision: or to assert that the manner in which they respond to it is against their long-run interest and that they would be in some sense better off if they should go against their deep-felt preferences. If their rationale for their decision behavior is not uniquely compelling. . . . , neither, it seems to me, are the counterarguments. Indeed, it seems out of the question summarily to judge their behavior as irrational: I am included among them.

In any case, it follows from the propositions above that for their behavior in the situations in question, the Bayesian or Savage approach gives wrong predictions and, by their lights, bad advice. They act in conflict with the axioms deliberately, without apology, because it seems to them the sensible way to behave. Are they clearly mistaken?

As with Berger, Ellsberg's language expresses the actualist perspective that what matters is the performance of a decision criterion in practice. He writes that if behavior conflicts with the Savage axioms, we should not conclude that decision makers are irrational. We should instead investigate the performance of the decision criteria they use to cope with ambiguity. He explicitly raises concern with "the nature of actual or 'successful' decision-making under uncertainty."

The Quest for Rationality and the Search for Certitude

I have stated previously that, as I see the matter, there is no unambiguously correct way to choose among undominated actions. Hence, I view as misguided the quest by Savage and other axiomatic decision theorists to prescribe some unique process of rational decision making with partial knowledge. We must face up to the nonexistence of optimal decision criteria and suffice with reasonable ones.

The quest for rationality has much in common with the search for certitude discussed in the first part of this book. Analysts often predict outcomes with certitude, even though the certitude is not credible. Similarly, decision theorists sometimes declare that they know the best way to make decisions, even though optimality is unattainable. I wrote in the Introduction that I hope to move future policy analysis away from incredible certitude and toward honest portrayal of partial knowledge. I similarly hope to move policy making toward honest recognition that multiple decision criteria may be reasonable.

5

⟹◆⟸

Diversified Treatment Choice

THIS chapter applies the framework for planning with partial knowledge introduced in Chapter 4 to the problem of allocating a population to two treatments. I also consider collective decision processes, where a group of policy makers jointly choose treatments. In both settings, I propose diversified treatment choice as a strategy to cope with uncertainty and reduce it over time. I originally developed this idea in Manski (2007a, 2009).

Financial diversification has long been a familiar recommendation for portfolio allocation, where an investor allocates wealth across a set of investments. A portfolio is said to be diversified if the investor allocates positive fractions of wealth to different investments, rather than all to one investment. An investor with full knowledge of the returns to alternative investments would not diversify. He would be better off investing all his wealth in the investment with the highest return. The rationale for financial diversification arises purely from incompleteness of knowledge. Broadly speaking, diversification enables someone who is uncertain about the returns to investments to balance different potential errors.

I will argue that diversification may also be appealing when a society must treat a population of persons and does not know the best treatment. I gave an initial example in Chapter 4 when the minimax-regret criterion was applied to the problem of treating x-pox. We found that a planner using this decision criterion would randomly assign half the population to each treatment. An individual could not diversify her own treatment. Each person received one treatment and either lived or died. Yet the community could diversify by having positive fractions of the population receive each treatment. Thus, private diversification of treatment for x-pox was impossible, but communal diversification was possible.

Sequential treatment of new cohorts of persons strengthens the appeal of diversification. The reason is that society may now benefit from learning, with observation of the outcomes experienced by earlier cohorts informing treatment choice for later cohorts. Diversification is advantageous for learning because it randomly assigns persons to the two treatments and thus yields the advantages for policy analysis of classical randomized experiments. In a stable environment where treatment response does not vary over time, diversification copes with uncertainty in the short run and reduces it in the long run.

Of course diversification is not always feasible. Humanity faces collective threats ranging from strategic nuclear war to systemic financial crisis to global warming to pandemics. As long as we inhabit just one integrated world, these risks are undiversifiable. Nevertheless, many risks are diversifiable. These are our present concern.

I first consider settings in which a planner treats a single cohort of persons. I then suppose that the planner sequentially treats a succession of cohorts of persons who have the same distribution of treatment response. Finally, the chapter considers collective decision processes.

For simplicity, I focus mainly on settings in which one treatment is a status quo and the other is an innovation. For example, the status quo may be a standard medical practice using existing technology, while the innovation may use new technology. It often is reasonable to suppose that response to a status quo treatment is known from experience. Then the only informational problem is partial knowledge of response to the innovation, which has not yet been used in practice.

Diversification and Profiling

Before we proceed, I should explain how treatment diversification differs from profiling. Diversification calls for randomly differential treatment of persons. Profiling, discussed in Chapter 4 in the context of police search, calls for systematically differential treatment of persons who differ in observable attributes thought to be associated with treatment response. For example, prescribed medical treatments may vary with patient age and health status. Public assistance to unemployed workers may vary with worker experience and skills. Sentencing of offenders may vary with prior convictions.

Profiling may be good policy when a planner knows something about how treatment response varies across groups of persons. If he knows that a particular treatment tends to work better for members of one group and a different treatment for those in another group, then he may want to systematically vary treatments across the two groups.

Diversification may be appealing when a planner does not know how treatment response varies across persons. Then he cannot systematically differentiate treatment. Yet he may find it beneficial to randomly vary treatment in order to cope with uncertainty and learn.

5.1. Allocating a Population to Two Treatments

When considering choice among undominated actions in Chapter 4, I distinguished situations in which a decision maker does and does not feel able to place subjective probabilities on the states of nature he thinks feasible. The expected welfare criterion has commonly been prescribed for decision making in the former situation. The maximin and minimax-regret criteria have been proposed for the latter situation.

The x-pox illustration showed that the decision criterion is consequential. Supposing that welfare is measured by the survival rate of the community, we found that a planner maximizing expected welfare does not diversify treatment. One using the maximin criterion diversifies with a 50–50 allocation in the example with two states of nature but not in the case with three states of nature. A planner using the minimax-regret criterion chooses a 50–50 allocation in both cases.

I show here how treatment choice depends on the decision criterion when a planner must assign each member of a population to one of two feasible treatments. As earlier, the two treatments are labeled A and B. As in the x-pox illustration, the feasible actions are treatment allocations, assigning a fraction of the population to each treatment. That is, for any allocation d between zero and one, the planner can assign fraction d of the population to treatment B and the remaining $1-d$ to A. As in the illustration, treatment response is individualistic.

The present analysis is simple enough that I can give a mostly self-contained exposition, using only elementary notation and algebra. (Readers who are averse to any algebra can read this section lightly and then proceed to Section 5.2.) Yet it generalizes the x-pox illustration in two important respects. First, the outcome of treatment may be a magnitude rather than a dichotomy such as survival versus death. Second, treatment response may vary across the population. For example, the outcome of interest for medical treatment may be the number of years that a patient survives. Persons who receive a given treatment may survive different lengths of time.

Treatment choice depends on the welfare function. In the x-pox illustration, welfare was measured by the survival rate of the population. Thus, the planner added up the 0–1 survival outcomes of each member of the population and divided by population size. A natural generalization of this idea is to let welfare be measured by the mean outcome of treatment. Thus, I will suppose that the planner adds up the outcomes of the population and divides by population size.

As in the x-pox illustration, the expected welfare, maximin, and minimax-regret criteria have distinct diversification properties. A planner maximizing expected welfare does not diversify treatment. One using the maximin criterion diversifies when the state space has certain properties but more typically does not diversify. A planner using the minimax-regret criterion always diversifies, the specific allocation depending on the mean treatment outcomes that he thinks feasible. Thus, the decision criterion that a planner uses is highly consequential for treatment choice.

The Welfare Function

To initiate the analysis, let $W(d, s)$ denote the welfare that results if the planner randomly assigns fraction d of the population to treatment B and state of nature s occurs. For example, if the outcome of interest for medical treatment is life span, $W(d, s)$ is the mean life span of the population of patients when fraction d of them receive treatment B and fraction $1 - d$ receive A.

We can write $W(d, s)$ as a weighted average of the mean outcomes that would occur if everyone were to receive one of the two treatments. $W(0, s)$ is the mean outcome that would occur if everyone were to receive treatment *A* and $W(1, s)$ is the mean outcome if everyone were to receive *B*. The mean outcome when fraction *d* of the population receive treatment *B* is *d* times $W(1, s)$ plus $(1 - d)$ times $W(0, s)$. Thus,

$$W(d, s) = (1 - d) \times W(0, s) + d \times W(1, s).$$

The planner wants to choose an allocation that maximizes this welfare function. The difficulty is that he does not know the true state of nature. All treatment allocations are undominated if there exists a state of nature *s* in which treatment *A* outperforms *B*, and another state *t* in which *B* outperforms *A*. To see this, compare any two fractions *c* and *d*, with *c* larger than *d*. Assigning fraction *c* of the population to treatment *B* outperforms assigning *d* in state *t*, but it underperforms *d* in state *s*.

A Status Quo Treatment and an Innovation

Having specified the welfare function, we can study treatment choice. To simplify the analysis, I henceforth let *A* be a status quo treatment and *B* an innovation. I suppose that the planner observes past response to *A* and finds it credible to assume that future response will remain the same. Thus, the planner knows the mean outcome that would occur if everyone were to receive treatment *A*, and he has partial knowledge only about response to *B*. I give the main results here and elaborate in Appendix B. Appendix C describes how the analysis extends to settings with partial knowledge of the outcomes of both treatments.

Let W_0 denote the known mean outcome that would occur if everyone were to receive the status quo treatment. Thus, the planner knows that $W(0, s) = W_0$ in every feasible state of nature. Then the welfare function takes the form

$$W(d, s) = (1 - d) \times W_0 + d \times W(1, s).$$

Let $L(1)$ and $H(1)$ denote the lowest and highest values that $W(1, s)$ takes across all feasible states. If $L(1) < W_0 < H(1)$, the planner does not know which treatment is best. Assigning everyone to the innovation may yield lower or higher welfare than assigning everyone to the status quo.

We are now ready to determine the treatment allocation chosen by a planner who uses the expected welfare, maximin, or minimax-regret criterion. I do so and then give two illustrations.

Expected Welfare

A planner using the expected welfare criterion places a subjective probability distribution on the states of nature that he thinks feasible. He uses this distribution to predict the welfare that would result if everyone were assigned to the innovation, weighting states of nature by their subjective probabilities. It can be shown that if he places high probability on states in which the innovation is more effective than the status quo, he assigns everyone to the innovation. Contrariwise, if he places low subjective probability on these states, he assigns everyone to the status quo.

Maximin

A planner using the maximin criterion evaluates the welfare from assigning everyone to the innovation by its lowest possible value, this being $L(1)$. If $L(1)$ is less than W_0, he assigns everyone to the status quo. Thus, the maximin criterion operationalizes a strong form of *status quo deference*, assigning the entire population to it unless the planner is certain that the innovation is better.

Minimax Regret

The maximin criterion is grossly asymmetric in its attitude toward treatment errors. It entirely avoids type B errors (choosing the innovation when the status quo is better), but it entirely ignores type A errors (choosing the status quo when the innovation is better). There is no intrinsic reason why one should view the two types of error asymmetrically. Suppose instead that the planner gives equal weight to type A and type B errors and, consequently, wants to balance their potential welfare effects. The minimax-regret criterion formalizes this idea.

The regret of a treatment allocation is the loss in welfare resulting from choice of this allocation rather than the best allocation. A planner would like to choose the best allocation, in which case regret would be zero. However, the planner does not know the best allocation. As discussed in Chapter 4, the minimax-regret criterion selects an allocation that minimizes the maximum regret that could potentially materialize.

I show in Appendix B that when $L(1) < W_0 < H(1)$, a planner using the minimax-regret criterion randomly assigns to the innovation this fraction of the population:

$$d = \frac{H(1) - W_0}{H(1) - L(1)}.$$

Observe that the fraction assigned to the innovation depends on the position of W_0 relative to $L(1)$ and $H(1)$. Given values for $L(1)$ and $H(1)$, the fraction receiving the innovation rises from zero to one as W_0 falls from $H(1)$ to $L(1)$. This variation is sensible. As W_0 falls, the maximum welfare loss from type A errors increases and that from type B errors decreases. Balancing the potential welfare effects of the two types of error requires that d increase.

Choosing Sentences for Convicted Juvenile Offenders

To illustrate planning with the expected welfare, maximin, and minimax-regret criteria, I will again use the Manski and Nagin study of judicial sentencing of convicted offenders. Let the planner be the state of Utah, and let the population under treatment be males under age sixteen who are convicted of an offense. Let treatment A be the status quo, this being judicial discretion to sentence an offender to residential confinement or to order a sentence that does not involve confinement. (This differs from Chapter 2, where treatment A was mandatory non-confinement.) As in Chapter 2, let treatment B be an innovation mandating confinement for all convicted offenders. Let welfare be measured by the fraction of offenders who refrain from committing a crime in the two-year period following sentencing.

Analyzing data on outcomes under the status quo, Manski and Nagin find that $W_0 = 0.39$. In the absence of knowledge of how judges choose sentences or how offenders respond to their sentences, the data reveal only that the fraction of offenders who would remain crime-free under the innovation is at least 0.03 but no greater than 0.92. Thus, $L(1) = 0.03$, and $H(1) = 0.92$.

Consider treatment choice with this partial knowledge. If the state of Utah maximizes expected welfare, it fully adopts the innovation of mandatory confinement if its subjective probability distribution on the state space makes the expected welfare of mandatory confinement exceed 0.39. It leaves the status quo of judicial discretion in place if the expected welfare of the innovation is less than 0.39.

If Utah uses the maximin criterion, it leaves the status quo in place because $L(1) = 0.03$ and $W_0 = 0.39$. If the state uses the minimax-regret criterion, it assigns a randomly chosen fraction $(0.92 - 0.39)/$ $(0.92 - 0.03) = 0.60$ of offenders to mandatory confinement, leaving judicial discretion in place for the remaining fraction 0.40.

Allocation of Wealth to a Safe and Risky Investment

A second illustration concerns financial rather than public planning. A familiar problem in financial planning is allocation of wealth between two investments, one safe and the other risky. The investor wants to maximize the rate of return on his portfolio. He knows the return to the safe investment, but he has only partial knowledge of the return to the risky one. He thinks that the risky investment may yield either a lower or a higher return than the safe one.

This decision problem has the same structure as treatment choice. The investor is a planner. Dollars of wealth are the population members. The safe and risky investments are treatments A and B respectively. A portfolio is a treatment allocation. The rate of return on a portfolio is welfare.

An investor using the expected welfare criterion computes the subjective expected return on the risky investment. He allocates all wealth to this investment if its expected return exceeds the known return on the safe investment. He allocates all wealth to the safe investment if the expected return on the risky investment is smaller than the known return on the safe investment.

An investor using the maximin criterion allocates all wealth to the safe investment. One using the minimax-regret criterion chooses a diversified portfolio, the fraction of wealth allocated to the risky investment being

$$\frac{H(1) - W_0}{H(1) - L(1)}.$$

In this application, W_0 is the known rate of return on the safe investment. The quantities $L(1)$ and $H(1)$ are the lowest and highest rates of return on the risky investment that the investor thinks possible.

Risk-Averse Planning

The findings described above depend on the premise that welfare is measured by the mean outcome of treatment. Thus, each unit change in the mean outcome yields the same change in welfare. In some settings, one may feel that each additional unit increase in the mean outcome adds less to welfare. This idea is familiar in analysis of financial planning. Researchers often suppose that reducing the return on a portfolio by 1 percent subtracts more from an investor's welfare than raising the return by 1 percent adds to welfare. Similarly, in the x-pox illustration, one may feel that reducing the survival rate of the population by 1 percent subtracts more from welfare than raising the survival rate by 1 percent adds to welfare.

How does revising the welfare function in this way affect treatment choice? The answer depends on the decision criterion. In expected utility theory, an investor who wants to maximize his portfolio return is said to be *risk neutral*. One who values a dollar lost more than a dollar earned is said to be *risk averse*. A classical result is that a risk-neutral investor will invest all of his wealth in the investment with the higher expected return, but a risk-averse investor may choose a diversified portfolio. Similarly, a risk-neutral planner will assign all members of the population to the treatment with the higher expected welfare, but a risk-averse planner may diversify treatment.

Example: Consider the x-pox scenario. Suppose that a planner places subjective probability $p(s)$ on the state of nature in which treatment A is effective, and $p(t)$ on the state in which B is effective, the probabilities summing to one. Let welfare be measured by the logarithm of the population survival rate—this welfare function values a life lost more than a life saved. Then the expected welfare criterion yields a treatment allocation that mirrors the planner's subjective probabilities. It can be shown that he assigns fraction $p(s)$ of the population to treatment A and fraction $p(t)$ to B.

The terms "risk neutral" and "risk averse" are specific to expected utility theory. However, the idea that each additional unit increase in mean outcome adds less to welfare is meaningful more generally. Hence, we can ask how an investor or planner who feels this way would behave when using the maximin or minimax-regret criterion.

I show in Manski (2009) that the minimax-regret portfolio choice or treatment allocation typically changes, but it remains diversified. In contrast, the maximin treatment allocation does not change. If $L(0) < W_0$, an investor using the maximin criterion always invests fully in the safe asset, and a planner always allocates everyone to the status quo treatment.

5.2. Diversification and Equal Treatment of Equals

Proposing that an investor may want to choose a diversified portfolio is uncontroversial. It is similarly uncontroversial to suggest that a firm diversify when making production decisions. For example, it is common to recommend that a farmer diversify when planting crops. In this setting, the treatments are alternative crops, the population comprises a set of plots of land, and the farmer may be uncertain about crop yields or prices.

I have, however, found it controversial to propose diversification of treatments to humans. Presenting the idea in seminars and lectures, I have frequently received comments that, in the absence of knowledge of treatment response that justifies profiling, all persons should receive the same treatment. The concern is that treatment diversification violates the ethical principle calling for "equal treatment of equals."

Section 5.1 did not address this ethical concern. When specifying the welfare function used by the planner, I maintained the traditional *consequentialist* assumption of public economics. That is, policy choices matter only for the outcomes they yield. Equal treatment of equals is a *deontological* consideration. That is, it supposes that actions have intrinsic value, apart from their consequences. I will address the concern with equal treatment here.

Ex Ante and Ex Post Equal Treatment

Diversification is consistent with the equal-treatment principle in the *ex ante* sense that all members of the population have the same probability of receiving a particular treatment. It violates the principle in the *ex post* sense that different persons ultimately receive different treatments. Thus, equal treatment holds ex ante but not ex post.

The x-pox scenario dramatically illustrates the difference between the ex ante and ex post senses of equal treatment. Administering treatment *A* to the entire population provides equal treatment in both senses. Moreover, it equalizes realized outcomes, as the entire population either survives or dies. Administering each treatment to half the population treats everyone equally ex ante, each person having a 50 percent chance of receiving each treatment. However, it does not treat people equally ex post. Nor does it equalize outcomes, as half the population lives and half dies.

Democratic societies ordinarily adhere to the ex post sense of equal treatment. Americans who have the same income, deductions, and exemptions are required to pay the same federal income tax. The Equal Protection clause in the Fourteenth Amendment to the U.S. Constitution is held to mean that all persons in a jurisdiction are subject to the same laws, not that all persons have the same chance of being subject to different laws.

Nevertheless, some important policies adhere to the ex ante sense of equal treatment but explicitly violate the ex post sense. American examples include random tax audits, drug testing and airport screening, random calls for jury service, and the Green Card and Vietnam draft lotteries. These policies have not been prompted by the desire to cope with uncertainty that motivates treatment diversification. Yet they do indicate some willingness of society to accept policies that provide ex ante equal but ex post unequal treatment.

Democratic societies come closer to treatment diversification as suggested here when they permit performance of randomized experiments. Randomized experiments are undertaken explicitly to learn about treatment response. Combining ex ante equal treatment with ex post unequal treatment is precisely what makes randomized experiments informative. Modern medical ethics permits randomization only under conditions of *clinical equipoise*—that is, when partial knowledge of treatment response prevents a determination that one treatment is superior to another.

The current practice of randomized experiments differs from treatment diversification mainly in that democracies do not ordinarily compel participation in experiments. Concern with compulsion has been particularly strong in medical trials, which advertise for volunteers and go to lengths to obtain informed consent from experimental subjects.

Combining Consequentialism and Deontological Ethics

Suppose that a society is concerned with the ex post sense of equal treatment but also wants to consider policies that diversify treatment. How might it proceed?

Philosophers often take the position that deontological considerations should supersede consequentialist ones. This suggests a lexicographic decision process in which one first restricts attention to actions deemed deontologically acceptable and only then considers the consequences of these actions. If one considers ex post unequal treatment to be unacceptable, diversification of treatment is off the table.

In contrast, economists almost universally think it permissible to make trade-offs, weighing the pros and cons of an action. Working from this perspective, I have suggested amending the welfare function of Section 5.1 by adding a term that expresses societal concern with ex post equal treatment (Manski 2009).

The idea is to let the welfare function have this form:

$$W(d, s) = (1 - d) \times W(0, s) + d \times W(1, s) - E(d),$$

where E expresses the social cost of deviating from equal treatment—that is, $E(0)$ and $E(1)$ equal zero but $E(d)$ is positive when d does not equal zero or one. Thus, one subtracts something from welfare when the allocation diversifies treatments. I considered the special case where $E(d)$ equals some positive constant for all diversified allocations and showed that concern with ex post equal treatment does not affect the minimax-regret allocation if the positive constant is not too large. However, the planner chooses to assign everyone to the same treatment if the magnitude of the constant exceeds a threshold.

A planner using such a welfare function trades off consequentialist and deontological considerations. He chooses a deontologically inferior allocation if it yields sufficiently superior outcomes.

5.3. Adaptive Diversification

I have so far supposed that the planner makes a onetime decision on treatment allocation. Now suppose that the planner sequentially treats a succession of cohorts. Sequential planning makes it possible to benefit from empirical learning, with observation of the outcomes experienced by earlier cohorts informing treatment choice for later cohorts.

The consequentialist argument for treatment diversification strengthens if a planner treats a sequence of cohorts of persons who have the same distribution of treatment response. Diversification generates randomized experiments yielding outcome data on both treatments. As time passes, the planner can revise his treatment allocation, treating successive cohorts differently as data accumulates. I call this idea *adaptive diversification*.

Adaptive Minimax Regret

The *adaptive minimax-regret* (AMR) criterion offers a simple way to implement adaptive diversification. The planner applies to each cohort the minimax-regret criterion using the knowledge of treatment response available at the time of treatment. The result is a diversified allocation whenever the available knowledge does not suffice to determine which treatment is better. The criterion is adaptive because knowledge of treatment response accumulates over time, so successive cohorts may receive different allocations. Eventually, the planner may learn which treatment is better. From this point on, he assigns new cohorts entirely to the better treatment.

The AMR criterion treats each cohort as well as possible, in the minimax-regret sense, given the available knowledge. It does not ask the members of one cohort to sacrifice their own welfare for the sake of learning. Nevertheless, use of the criterion enables learning that benefits future cohorts.

Implementation in Centralized Health Care Systems

If concern with ex post equal treatment does not preclude treatment diversification, the AMR criterion can be implemented in centralized health care systems where government agencies directly assign treatments. Examples include the National Health Service in the United Kingdom and the Military Health System in the United States.

To illustrate how this might work in practice, let *A* be a status quo treatment for a life-threatening disease and let *B* be an innovation. Let

Table 5.1   AMR choice of treatment

Cohort n or year k	Fraction of cohort 0 surviving k^{th} year after treatment		Bound on $W(1)$, cohort n	AMR allocation, cohort n	Mean years of survival, cohort n
	Status quo	Innovation			
0			[0, 4]	0.325	2.83
1	0.8	0.9	[0.9, 3.6]	0.333	2.83
2	0.7	0.8	[1.7, 3.3]	0.375	2.85
3	0.6	0.7	[2.4, 3.1]	0.571	2.93
4	0.6	0.7	[3.1, 3.1]	1	3.10

the outcome of interest be the number of years that a person survives in a four-year horizon following treatment. Let welfare be measured by the mean number of years of survival.

Table 5.1 shows the AMR treatment allocation each year in a scenario where the fraction of persons receiving the status quo treatment who survive one through four years are (0.8, 0.7, 0.6, 0.6) respectively, implying a mean of 2.7 years. The corresponding fractions under the innovation are (0.9, 0.8, 0.7, 0.7) years, implying a mean of 3.1 years. The planner knows from experience that the mean number of years of survival under the status quo treatment is 2.7 years. However, he has no initial knowledge of the effectiveness of the innovation—the mean number of years of survival could be anything from 0 to 4 years. Then the initial AMR treatment allocation assigns the fraction $(4-2.7)/(4-0) = 0.325$ of all persons to the innovation.

A year later, the planner observes that 0.9 of the persons receiving the innovation survive the first year after treatment. Then he can conclude that the mean number of years of survival under the innovation is at least 0.9 and at most 3.6 years. Hence, the updated AMR allocation to the innovation is $(3.6-2.7)/(3.6-0.9) = 0.333$. The planner learns more from observing outcomes in years two through four, and further updates the AMR allocation to 0.375, 0.571, and 1 respectively.

The specific sequence of AMR allocations shown in the table results from the specific sequence of realized outcomes under the two treatments. The broad message illustrated by the table is that, as information accumulates, the AMR criterion eventually allocates the entire population to the better treatment.

The AMR Criterion and the Practice of Randomized Clinical Trials

The illustration of table 5.1 exemplifies a host of settings in which a health planner must choose between a well-understood status quo treatment and an innovation whose properties are only partially known. When facing situations of this kind, it has been common to perform RCTs to learn about the innovation. The fractional allocations produced by the AMR criterion yield randomized experiments, so it is natural to ask how application of the AMR criterion differs from the current practice of RCTs. There are several major differences. I describe three here, continuing the discussion of FDA drug approval begun in Chapter 1.

Fraction of the Population Receiving the Innovation

The AMR criterion can in principle yield any fractional treatment allocation. In contrast, the group receiving the innovation in current RCTs is typically a very small fraction of the relevant population. In trials conducted to obtain FDA approval of new drugs, the sample receiving the innovation typically comprises two to three thousand persons, whereas the relevant patient population may contain hundreds of thousands or millions of persons. Thus, the fraction of the population receiving the innovation is generally less than 0.01 and often less than 0.001.

Group Subject to Randomization

Under the AMR criterion, the persons receiving the innovation are randomly drawn from the full patient population. In contrast, present clinical trials randomly draw subjects from pools of persons who volunteer to participate. Hence, a trial at most reveals the distribution of treatment response within the subpopulation of volunteers, not within the full patient population.

Measurement of Outcomes

Under the AMR criterion, one observes the health outcomes of real interest as they unfold over time, and one uses these data to inform subsequent treatment decisions. In contrast, the trials performed to obtain FDA approval of new drugs typically have durations of only two to three years.

Attempting to learn from trials of short duration, medical researchers often measure surrogate outcomes rather than outcomes of real interest. Medical researchers have cautioned that extrapolation from surrogate outcomes to outcomes of interest can be difficult (see Fleming and Demets 1996 and Psaty et al. 1999). Nevertheless, the practice persists.

5.4. Diversification across Time or Space

Sections 5.1 through 5.3 contemplated a planner having full power to assign treatments. This section and the next concern planners with more-limited powers. Here I consider ones who cannot differentially treat individual members of the population but who can assign or influence the treatments of groups who are separated in time or space. Such planners have some ability to adaptively diversify treatment.

Diversification by Cohort

Suppose that a planner cannot diversify treatment within the cohort of persons who must be treated in the same month, year, or another specified period. The reason may be a legal requirement for ex post equal treatment of equals. Or it may be a technical constraint on the administration of treatments. Such a planner may perhaps find it feasible to diversify across cohorts separated in time.

For example, the health planner considered in table 5.1 might assign everyone in the cohort of year 0 to treatment A, all members of cohort 1 to treatment B, all of cohort 3 to A, and so on. Continuing in this manner, the planner could sequentially achieve various long-run treatment allocations. In the five-year context of table 5.1, the planner could make the total fraction of persons assigned to treatment B take any of these values: 0, 0.2, 0.4, 0.6, 0.8, or 1.

Diversification by cohort is not as flexible as diversification within cohorts. However, if treatment response does not vary over time, it eventually achieves the same benefits. It enables a planner to cope with ambiguity and to learn about treatment response.

Laboratories of Democracy

The Constitution of the United States gives the federal government limited power to set policy, reserving much discretion to the states. However, American federalism does not preclude a rough approximation to adaptive diversification.

The American Progressive movement has long appreciated that federalism enables the states to experiment with new policy ideas. A century ago, Theodore Roosevelt (1912), wrote this about Senator Robert La Follette:

> Thanks to the movement for genuinely democratic popular government which Senator La Follette led to overwhelming victory in Wisconsin, that state has become literally a laboratory for wise experimental legislation aiming to secure the social and political betterment of the people as a whole.

Twenty years later, Supreme Court justice Louis Brandeis, in his dissent to the 1932 case *New York State Ice Co. v. Liebmann* (285 U.S. 311), added what has become a famous remark on this theme:

> It is one of the happy incidents of the federal system that a single courageous State may, if its citizens choose, serve as a laboratory; and try novel social and economic experiments without risk to the rest of the country.

It has since become common to refer to the states as the *laboratories of democracy.*

The Roosevelt and Brandeis statements clearly appreciate that policy variation across states can enable learning about treatment response. Such variation is broadly similar to diversification by cohorts, the cohorts here being separated by space rather than time. A caveat is that policy variation across states ordinarily is not the result of purposeful randomization. Extrapolation of findings from one state to another requires one to assume that states with different policies have similar distributions of treatment response. The credibility of this assumption may vary with the context.

While federalism empowers the states to choose their own policies in certain domains, it does not require that the federal government remain passive as this occurs. The federal government can provide incentives to the states to encourage them to enact desirable portfolios of policies. Thus, the federal government can encourage adaptive diversification across states, modifying the incentives as knowledge of treatment response accumulates. The federal government played such an active role in welfare policy in the late 1980s, when it encouraged states to institute and evaluate variations on the then-existing program of Aid to Families with Dependent Children (see Greenberg and Wiseman 1992 and Fishman and Weinberg 1992).

5.5. Adaptive Partial Drug Approval

Apart from the Military Health System and some other entities serving specific subpopulations, the largely decentralized American health care system does not give planners the power to directly assign medical treatments. Nevertheless, there are ways to partially implement the broad theme of adaptive diversification.

I will use the regulatory process of drug approval to suggest some of what might be accomplished. In Chapter 1, I observed that the Food and Drug Administration makes considerable use of conventional certitudes when it attempts to extrapolate from clinical-trial data to predict the effectiveness and safety of new drugs in practice. A process of *adaptive partial drug approval* could improve on current FDA practice.

The Present Approval Process

Although the FDA was created over a century ago in the Pure Food and Drug Act of 1906, the present drug approval process is a more recent invention. Until 1938, the agency was unable to disapprove the sale of purported medicines. It only was able to outlaw labeling and other advertising that made unsupported claims of safety and effectiveness. The Food, Drug, and Cosmetics Act (FDCA) of 1938 gave the FDA power to prohibit the sale of unsafe drugs, but without a requirement to assess effectiveness. The 1962 Amendments to the FDCA established the modern process, which requires pharmaceutical firms to demonstrate that new drugs are safe and effective through a series of RCTs.

The present process begins with laboratory and animal testing of new compounds. Those that seem promising then go through three phases of RCTs, in which the new drug is compared with an accepted treatment or placebo. Phase 1 trials, which typically take a year and are performed with twenty to eighty healthy volunteers, aim to determine the basic pharmacological action of the drug and the safety of different doses. Phase 2 trials, which usually take two years and are performed with several hundred volunteers who are ill with a specific disease, give preliminary evidence on the effectiveness and short-term side effects of the drug. Phase 3 trials, which usually take three years and are performed with several hundred to several thousand volunteers ill with the disease, give further evidence on effectiveness and side effects. Following completion of Phase 3, the firm files a New Drug Application. The FDA then either approves or disapproves the drug after reviewing the findings of the trials.

FDA evaluation of New Drug Applications occurs with partial knowledge of treatment response. As a consequence, drug approval decisions are susceptible to two types of errors. A type B error occurs when a new drug that is actually inferior to a status quo is approved because it appears superior when evaluated using the available information. A type A error occurs when a new drug that is actually superior to the status quo is disapproved because it appears inferior when evaluated using the available information. Some type B errors eventually are corrected after approval through the FDA's post-market surveillance program, which analyzes data on the outcomes experienced when the drug is used in clinical practice. Type A errors often are permanent, because after a drug is disapproved, use of the drug ceases and no further data on treatment response are produced.

The length of the FDA process has long been debated. Pharmaceutical firms and patient advocates wanting fast access to new drugs argue for shortening the process. Health researchers and patient advocates concerned that approval decisions are made with inadequate knowledge of treatment response argue that trials of longer duration should be performed on subjects who more closely resemble patient populations. The columnist Anne Applebaum aptly described the periodic ebb and flow of these arguments as "The Drug Approval Pendulum" (Applebaum 2005).

Attention has focused on the length of the approval process because the permitted use of a new drug has a sharp discontinuity at the date of the FDA approval decision. Beforehand, a typically tiny fraction of the patient population receives the new drug in clinical trials. Afterward, use of the drug is unconstrained if approval is granted and zero if approval is not granted. Thus, the date of the approval decision is a central feature of the process.

Binary versus Partial Approval

The FDA practice of framing approval as a binary (yes/no) decision between full approval and complete disapproval needlessly constrains the set of policy options. Our discussion of adaptive diversification suggests that it may be beneficial to empower the FDA to institute an adaptive partial approval process, where the extent of the permitted use of a new drug would vary as evidence accumulates. The stronger the evidence on outcomes of interest, the more that use of a new drug would be permitted.

To see why adaptive partial approval can improve on the present process, consider the sharp discontinuity in drug availability pre- and post-approval. A new drug is essentially unavailable to the patient population before the approval decision, being obtainable only through participation in a clinical trial and even then only when randomly assigned to a subject. From a social welfare perspective, it is not evident that uncertainty about the relative merits of the status quo and an innovation should result in a societal decision to treat almost the entire patient population with the status quo. To motivate this decision, one might appeal to the maximin criterion, under which one performs a worst-case analysis of the new drug and act as if the truth is this worst case. Or one might argue that society should place much more weight on type B errors than on type A errors. However, there is no inherent reason why society should act so conservatively or weigh the two types of error asymmetrically.

Suppose that society gives equal weight to type A and type B errors and consequently wants to balance their potential welfare effects. The minimax-regret criterion operationalizes this approach to treatment choice. Applying this criterion to choice between a status quo treatment and an innovation shows that it is best to diversify treatment by having a positive fraction of patients receive each treatment. The fraction receiving the new drug is chosen to balance its upside potential against its downside risk.

If the FDA had the power to assign treatments directly, it could implement the AMR criterion as described in Section 5.3. The initial allocation of patients to the status quo and the new drug would reflect the initial knowledge available about the effectiveness of the innovation. As evidence from trials accumulates, the FDA would revise the allocation accordingly. Eventually, the FDA would learn which treatment is best. At this point a binary approval decision would be made.

Adaptive Partial Licensing

The FDA does not have the power to mandate treatment. It can only place an upper bound on use of a drug by approving its production and marketing. In this legal setting, I suggest empowering the FDA to grant limited-term sales licenses while clinical trials are under way. A license would permit a firm seeking approval of a new drug to sell no more than a specified quantity over a specified period.

The duration of a license would depend on the schedule for reporting new findings in the trials. For example, if the firm reports updated outcome data to the FDA annually, then the licensing decision could be updated annually as well. On each iteration of the decision, the maximum quantity of drug that the firm is permitted to sell would be set by the FDA with the assistance of an expert advisory board, similar to those now used in drug approval. The task of the advisory board would be to assess the upside potential and downside risk of the new drug, given the information available at the time.

Under the new regime, clinical trials would usually be longer than at present, sometimes considerably longer. The reason is to measure health outcomes of real interest, thus reducing the present dependency of drug evaluation on surrogate outcomes. When the outcomes of interest have been observed, the FDA would make a binary approval decision. If the drug is deemed safe and effective, the firm would be permitted to sell it with no quantity restriction. Further use would be prohibited otherwise.

As in the current environment, the FDA would retain the right to rescind its approval should new evidence warrant. Post-market surveillance would be necessary, because lengthening clinical trials to measure outcomes of interest may not suffice to determine with certainty whether the innovation is superior to the status quo. As with present trials, the lengthened trials would only reveal treatment response for volunteer subjects who comply with treatment and do not drop out of the trial. Moreover, unless the FDA changes its norms on blinding treatment assignment, the trials would not reveal treatment response in real clinical settings where patients and physicians know the assigned treatments.

The approval process suggested here would not achieve all of the benefits of adaptive diversification, which calls for randomly allocating the entire patient population between the status quo treatment and the innovation. The new process would yield observational data on treatment response in the full patient population. These data would substantially add to the clinical trial data now available, but they would not be as informative as data produced by randomizing treatment of the entire patient population.

5.6. Collective Decision Processes

To motivate the study of planning with partial knowledge, I wrote at the beginning of Chapter 4 that policy choice in an uncertain world is subtle even when a society agrees on what it wants and what it believes. I observed that even such a cohesive society cannot make optimal policy decisions, at most reasonable ones. Our subsequent examination of various planning problems has demonstrated this generality. It has also provided several instances where the study of planning has practical application. While public agencies in democracies may not have absolute power to assign treatments, they do have constrained power to assign or influence treatments.

This section moves away from the idealization of a solitary planner and considers settings where a group collectively makes treatment decisions. The members of the decision group might be the citizens of a democratic society, an elected legislature, or an oligarchy. Whatever the group may be, the core new problem is heterogeneity in policy preferences.

A homogeneous decision group—one whose members share the same objective for society, have the same belief about policy outcomes, and use the same decision criterion to cope with uncertainty—would achieve consensus in policy choice. Collective decision making would be tantamount to choice by a solitary planner who represents the group. However, a famous *impossibility theorem* of Kenneth Arrow (1951) showed that if the members of the decision group have arbitrarily heterogeneous policy preferences, there exists no voting system or other non-dictatorial collective decision process that emulates a planner.

Condorcet's Paradox: Social choice theorists as early as the eighteenth-century French polymath Marquis de Condorcet have used majority-rule voting to illustrate the potential incoherence of collective decision processes. Suppose that there are three policy alternatives, labeled (*C*, *D*, *E*), and three members of the decision group, each with a different ranking of the policies. Suppose that one person ranks the policies from most preferred to least preferred in the order (*C* > *D* > *E*), another in the order (*D* > *E* > *C*), and the third in the order (*E* > *C* > *D*). Let the policies be compared pairwise. Then a majority of persons (two out of three) vote for *C* over *D*, a majority vote for *D* over *E*, and a majority vote for *E* over *C*. This result, called *Condorcet's paradox*, shows that majority-rule voting does not yield a clear social preference ordering if the decision group is sufficiently heterogeneous. Thus, majority rule cannot answer the question: Which policy is socially most preferred?

Arrow's impossibility theorem is sometimes interpreted as implying that it is hopeless to seek coherence in collective decision making. However, social choice theorists have subsequently sought to escape this nihilistic conclusion. They have observed that Arrow's theorem, like all deduction, rests on certain assumptions. In particular, it considers a decision group with arbitrarily heterogeneous policy preferences, not one whose members have some degree of commonality. Restricting the scope of heterogeneity can mitigate the negativity of Arrow's conclusion. I pursue this idea below, in the context of treatment allocation.

Majority-Rule Voting with Single-Peaked Preferences

Consider a decision process in which a group containing an odd number of members uses majority-rule voting to choose treatments for a population. The stipulation that the group has an odd number of members eliminates the possibility of tie votes. Institutions for collective decision making commonly frame treatment choice as a binary decision between two singleton allocations—assign everyone in the population to treatment *A* or everyone to *B*. However, legislatures and other decision groups may in principle be able to choose fractional treatment allocations.

Assume that each member of the group has *single-peaked* preferences. That is, each decision maker ranks some treatment allocation most highly and ranks other allocations by their ordinal proximity to the most preferred one. Then the *median-voter theorem* of Black (1948) shows that majority-rule voting yields the treatment allocation that would be chosen by a planner whose most preferred allocation is the median of the most preferred allocations of all voters. For short, this is called the preference of the median voter.

Black did not study treatment allocation per se. He considered an abstract class of problems in which alternative policies are ordered from smallest to largest, or from left to right. Treatment allocation is in this class, but it has not been a specific subject of study by social choice theorists. Researchers have typically applied the median-voter theorem to policies ordered from most liberal to most conservative.

To understand Black's result, suppose that decision makers are asked to vote pairwise on all alternative treatment allocations, say d and e, assigning a fraction d or e of the population to treatment B and the remainder to A. In each case majority rule is used to determine the winner. For example, they are asked to vote on allocation $d=0$ versus $e=1$, on $d=0$ versus $e=\frac{1}{2}$, on $d=\frac{1}{2}$ versus $e=\frac{3}{4}$, and so on. If preferences are single-peaked, the preferred allocation of the median voter will win all of the elections in which it appears, receiving a majority of the votes when compared pairwise against all alternatives. The reason is that, no matter what the alternative, at least half of the voters find that the allocation of the median voter is closer to their most preferred allocation than is the alternative.

The median-voter theorem does not contradict Arrow's impossibility theorem because single-peakedness restricts the class of permissible policy preferences. Persons with single-peaked preferences may vary arbitrarily in the location of their most preferred allocation. Some may most prefer that everyone receive treatment A, others may most prefer allocating everyone to B, and still others may most prefer allocating a positive fraction of the population to each treatment. However, single-peakedness does not allow certain policy preferences. In particular, it disallows preferences that enable majority-rule voting to produce no determinate ordering of policies.

The Credibility of Single-Peaked Preferences

Is it reasonable to suppose that a citizenry, legislature, or other decision group actually has single-peaked preferences for treatment allocations?

I have no empirical evidence on the matter, but the analysis earlier in this chapter is suggestive.

Consider choice between a status quo treatment and an innovation, discussed in Section 5.1. Suppose that the objective is to maximize the mean outcome of treatment. Then the expected welfare, maximin, and minimax-regret criteria all manifest single-peaked preferences. Expected welfare is maximized by assigning everyone to one treatment or the other, and it decreases as the allocation moves away from the peak. Minimum welfare is maximized by assigning everyone to the status quo, and it decreases as more persons are assigned to the innovation. Maximum regret is minimized at some fractional allocation, and it increases with distance from the most preferred allocation.

On the other hand, a deontological preference for ex post equal treatment of equals implies that preferences are not single-peaked. As discussed in Section 5.2, a person who cares about ex post equal treatment would rather assign everyone to the same treatment than assign almost everyone to one treatment and the remainder to the other. This violates single-peakedness.

Leaving aside preference for ex post equal treatment, suppose that all voters have single-peaked preferences. Then the median-voter theorem implies that majority-rule voting will assign the entire population to one treatment only if a majority of voters most prefer this allocation. The result will be diversification otherwise.

Suppose, for example, that 45 percent of the voters most prefer the status quo, 40 percent most prefer the innovation, and 15 percent most prefer some fractional allocation. Then the median voter prefers a fractional allocation. Majority rule yields diversification here even though relatively few voters most prefer a fractional allocation. This outcome may seem counterintuitive, but it has an attractive interpretation. In the example, voters are deeply split on their most preferred policy. With single-peaked preferences, a fractional allocation is a compromise that draws the most support when compared pairwise with any alternative.

Strategic Interactions

I have thus far assumed that decision makers vote their true policy preferences. This assumption is realistic when decision makers have no opportunity to influence one another, as in large electorates voting in isolation by secret ballot. However, it may not be realistic when there are opportunities for strategic interaction, as in legislatures and other settings where a relatively small electorate votes by open ballot.

In legislative and similar settings, decision makers may think it strategically advantageous not to vote in accord with their policy preferences. They may also think it advantageous to express incredible certitude, seeking to influence their colleagues' beliefs and those of the public. Seeking to avoid dueling certitudes, they may embrace conventional certitudes such as CBO scoring.

I can do no more than conjecture on how strategic interactions may affect legislative treatment choice. I see potential for two opposing forces. First, strategic expression of incredible certitude may inhibit diversification. A legislator who expresses certitude about policy outcomes should, to be consistent with his expressed beliefs, vote to assign everyone to one treatment.

Consider choice between a status quo treatment and an innovation. If a legislature votes to assign everyone to the status quo, it will obtain no empirical evidence on response to the innovation. This is fine if the legislature is correct in thinking that the status quo yields better outcomes than the innovation, but not if it acts based on incredible certitude. Misplaced certitude that the status quo is best can prevent society from ever learning the truth.

The opposing force is that strategic voting may promote fractional treatment allocation as a means for compromise among legislators with heterogeneous policy preferences. When the only options under consideration are to assign everyone to the same treatment, legislative action yields clear winners and losers. Broadening the feasible policies to include fractional allocations opens scope for partial achievement of legislative objectives—half a loaf is better than none. Fractional allocations that emerge in this manner are not intended to cope with uncertainty and hence are intellectually distinct from diversification. Nevertheless, they may achieve the benefits of diversification.

Learning and Heterogeneity of Policy Preferences

Now consider a multi-period allocation problem. As with a planner, a group using a voting system to make decisions may learn about treatment response from experience. This does not imply, however, that heterogeneity of policy preferences lessens over time. Learning promotes consensus when policy disagreements stem from differing beliefs, but it may increase polarization when disagreements stem from differing welfare functions. Consideration of two polar scenarios makes the point.

Suppose first that the members of the decision group share the same welfare function and use the same decision criterion but have different beliefs about policy outcomes. Then they may have different policy preferences, reflecting their heterogeneity of beliefs. However, learning about treatment response should make their beliefs converge, eventually yielding consensus on policy preferences.

Contrariwise, suppose that the group members share the same beliefs and decision criterion but evaluate outcomes with different welfare functions. Then learning generally will not yield consensus. Indeed, a consensus in the absence of knowledge may be replaced by stark disagreement when policy outcomes become known.

A striking example of this phenomenon is the Rawls (1971) application of the Harsanyi (1953) concept of a *veil of ignorance*. Rawls conjectured that if the members of a self-centered society were required to jointly choose a distribution of income under a veil of ignorance—that is, without knowing their relative positions in the distribution—they would all prefer an equal distribution of income. On the other hand, if they were required to jointly choose an income distribution while knowing their relative positions in it, they would sharply disagree. Each person's policy preferences would depend on his placement in the distribution. In particular, each would most prefer equal division of societal income to himself and the persons ranked above him in the distribution, leaving nothing for all those ranked below him.

The Rawls scenario cautions that a society with better knowledge of policy outcomes would not necessarily become a more cohesive society. However, it would be illogical to draw the contrary conclusion that knowledge is dangerous. The appropriate lesson is that the source of heterogeneity in policy preferences matters. Learning promotes consensus when policy disagreements stem from differing beliefs, but it may increase polarization when disagreements stem from conflicting objectives.

Bilateral Negotiations

When studying majority-rule voting, I considered a decision group with an odd number of members. This avoided having to ask how a policy is chosen in the event of a tie vote. Ties are a minor concern when studying voting by large groups with an even number of members, as they occur rarely in large electorates. However, they are the essence of the problem in bilateral negotiations, when the decision group contains two members. Then the only possible voting outcomes are consensus or a tie. Hence, majority-rule voting is not a useful decision process in bilateral negotiations.

Pareto Optimal Allocations

Game theory shows that prediction of the outcomes of bilateral negotiations is difficult in principle, and empirical researchers have found it challenging in practice. However, the concept of *partial optimality* yields partial predictions that may sometimes be credible and informative.

A collective decision process is said to be Pareto optimal (honoring the early Italian economist Vilfredo Pareto) if it respects consensus. That is, when the entire decision group agrees that policy C is preferable to D, the process chooses C over D. A policy is Pareto optimal if there exists no other policy that is preferred by all members of the group. Thus, Pareto optimality of a policy is a type of dominance. When studying a solitary planner, decision theory regards a policy as undominated if there exists no other policy that performs better in every state of nature. A Pareto optimal policy is undominated in the different sense that no other policy is preferred by every member of a decision group.

Social choice theorists and empirical researchers sometimes presume that, however a group makes joint decisions, it will choose a policy that is Pareto optimal. They reason that, whatever the group may do, the members will not choose a policy that makes them all worse off. This reasoning is not innocuous—the *prisoner's dilemma* is a well-known class of two-player game in which standard game theory predicts a Pareto inferior outcome. Nevertheless, theorists and empirical researchers often think it credible to assume that Pareto optimality will prevail in bilateral negotiations.

With this background, consider a bilateral negotiation on treatment allocation and suppose that the allocation preferences of both parties are single-peaked. Then the Pareto optimal allocations are those that lie in the interval connecting their most preferred allocations. For example, suppose that one party most prefers to allocate 30 percent of the population to treatment B and the other most prefers to allocate 40 percent to B. Now consider the allocations 20 percent, 35 percent, and 50 percent. Both parties prefer 30 percent over 20 percent, and both prefer 40 percent over 50 percent. On the other hand, there exists no alternative to 35 percent that both prefer. Hence, 35 percent is a Pareto optimal allocation, but 20 and 50 percent are not Pareto optimal.

Incentive-Compatible Processes

In Manski (2009), I proposed a decision process that encourages choice of a Pareto optimal allocation if both decision makers have single-peaked preferences. The context was choice between a status quo treatment and an innovation. The process first calls on each of the two parties to announce his most preferred allocation. It then uses either of two rules to choose the allocation.

One rule, expressing status quo deference, selects the announced allocation that assigns more persons to the status quo treatment. The other, expressing innovation deference, selects the announced allocation that assigns more persons to the innovation. I showed that both rules are *incentive compatible*. That is, both encourage each decision maker, considering his own policy preferences, to announce his most preferred allocation truthfully, regardless of what the other party announces.

While status quo deference and innovation deference both yield Pareto optimal and incentive-compatible decision processes, they may differ in their implications for learning. If both decision makers most prefer fractional allocations, then both processes yield a fractional allocation and hence enable learning about policy outcomes under the innovation. However, if some decision maker most prefers to assign everyone to the status quo, then only innovation deference enables learning. With status quo deference, no one is assigned to the innovation, and hence there is no opportunity for learning.

Teacher Evaluation in New York City

To illustrate bilateral negotiation, consider choice between a status quo policy for teacher evaluation and an innovation. The two decision makers are a school district and a teachers' union. The status quo is the traditional system basing evaluation on scrutiny of teacher preparation and observation of classroom lesson delivery. The innovation bases teacher evaluation on student performance in standardized tests. The contract between the school district and the union requires that any departure from the status quo be approved by both decision makers.

An instance of this teacher evaluation problem was described in an article in the *New York Times* (Medina 2008):

> New York City has embarked on an ambitious experiment, yet to be an-nounced, in which some 2,500 teachers are being measured on how much their students improve on annual standardized tests. . . . While officials say it is too early to determine how they will use the data, which is already being collected, they say it could eventually be used to help make decisions on teacher tenure or as a significant element in perfor-mance evaluations and bonuses. . . . Randi Weingarten, the union presi-dent, said she had grave reservations about the project, and would fight if the city tried to use the information for tenure or formal evaluations or even publicized it. She and the city disagree over whether such moves would be allowed under the contract.

Thus, New York City acted unilaterally to collect data that could poten-tially be used to evaluate teachers. The contemplated change from the status quo differs from a fractional allocation as defined in this book because the participating schools were not randomly drawn from the set of New York City schools. This difference aside, the allocation that the city had in mind was fractional, with about 10 percent of teachers assigned to the innovation.

New York City appeared to see itself as a solitary planner with uni-lateral power to implement the innovation. However, the teachers' union asserted that any departure from the status quo policy required their agreement. The *Times* reporter wrote that an attempted unilateral decision by the city "would undoubtedly open up a legal battle with the teacher's union."

Suppose that implementation of a new policy requires agreement by the city and the union. As originally framed, the negotiation consid-ered only two allocations, assigning all teachers to the status quo or assigning 10 percent to the innovation. My analysis suggests having the city and the union each announce its preferred allocation, followed by selection of the smaller of the announced allocations.

The fact that the city contemplated a fractional allocation suggests that it viewed itself as facing a problem of treatment choice under ambiguity. The union's perception was not apparent, because it had no way to voice its preference except to state its opposition to unilateral decision making by the city.

The union may have been certain that the status quo is better than the innovation. If so, incentive-compatible decision making with status quo deference would retain the status quo. However, the union and the city may have been sufficiently in sync that they both would prefer to diversify and learn. The incentive-compatible process would enable them to do so, through a negotiated implementation of adaptive diversification.

5.7. Laissez-Faire

To conclude this chapter I consider laissez-faire treatment choice as an alternative to planning. A long-standing concern of public economics has been to characterize the circumstances in which laissez-faire, self-selection of treatments by the treated, yields higher welfare than planning. Arguments for laissez-faire sometimes combine consequentialist welfare economics with a deontological preference for private decision making. I will approach the matter purely from the consequentialist perspective.

Laissez-faire is not sensible when public and private objectives diverge sharply. We would not want to have convicted offenders choose their own sentences or households choose their own income tax schedules. It may be appealing when public and private objectives are reasonably congruent. The prima facie argument for laissez-faire seems strongest when treatment response is individualistic and the social objective is to maximize utilitarian welfare. Then the relative merits of planning and laissez-faire depend on the relative effectiveness of society and private persons in achieving their common objectives.

A standard economic argument for laissez-faire combines two assumptions. First, it supposes that individuals know more about their treatment response than planners do. Hence, individuals are more able than planners to profile when making decisions. Second, it assumes that individuals have rational expectations. In combination, these assumptions imply that individuals make better treatment choices than a planner can.

However, economists typically make these assumptions without offering evidence of their realism. Do individuals actually know more about their treatment response than do planners? For example, do patients know more about their response to medical treatment than do physicians? In medical and other settings, it may be more reasonable to think that individuals and planners have overlapping but non-nested knowledge of treatment response.

Do individuals have rational expectations? That is, do they know the distribution of treatment response among persons who share their observable attributes? I stressed in Chapter 3 that individuals, like planners, confront difficult inferential problems as they seek to learn about treatment response. Hence, individuals and planners alike choose treatments with partial knowledge. If individuals are encumbered by psychological or cognitive limitations, their beliefs may be even more distant from rational expectations.

The bottom line is that one should be skeptical of broad assertions that individuals are better informed than planners and hence make better decisions. Of course, skepticism of such assertions does not imply that planning is more effective than laissez-faire. Their relative merits depend on the particulars of the choice problem. In a world replete with uncertainty, I am skeptical that it will ever be possible to draw general conclusions about the relative merits of planning and laissez-faire.

Social Learning from Private Experiences

While general conclusions may be infeasible, researchers can make progress studying particular classes of treatment-choice problems. To illustrate, I describe my theoretical study of laissez-faire choice between a status quo treatment and an innovation by a sequence of cohorts of persons who have partial knowledge of treatment response (Manski 2004b, 2005b).

Social scientists have long wanted to understand how individuals learn about and choose innovations. A common scenario envisions an initial condition in which only a status quo treatment is available. Persons know response to this treatment from experience. At some point, an innovation yielding unknown outcomes becomes available. From then on, successive cohorts of persons choose between the status quo treatment and the innovation, with later cohorts observing the experiences of earlier ones and learning from them. I called this dynamic process *social learning from private experiences.*

It has often been conjectured, and sometimes observed, that the fraction of decision makers choosing an innovation increases with time in the manner of an S-shaped curve—first rising slowly, then rapidly, and finally converging to some limit value (e.g., Griliches 1957). However, this is not the only possible dynamic for adoption of an innovation. The fraction of persons choosing the innovation could begin high and then decrease with time, or the time path could be non-monotone. My analysis showed that laissez-faire learning can generate potentially complex time paths for the adoption of innovations.

I supposed that individuals must choose their treatments at specific times and cannot revise their choices once made. Thus, they cannot undertake *learning-by-doing* and cannot otherwise wait for empirical evidence to accumulate before making decisions. This simplifying assumption implies that each person faces a single choice problem with predetermined information. Thus, dynamics emerge purely out of the process of social learning across successive cohorts. Individuals do not themselves face dynamic choice problems.

I assumed that successive cohorts have the same distribution of treatment response and are aware of this fact. This is the same invariance assumption that I made in Section 5.3 when considering adaptive diversification. It implies that empirical evidence accumulates over time, each successive cohort being able to draw inferences from a longer history of past experiences. I further assumed that persons have no prior knowledge of response to the innovation, nor about the decision processes of earlier cohorts. They only observe the treatments chosen by earlier cohorts and the outcomes that they experienced.

My basic finding on learning was that accumulation of empirical evidence over time successively narrows the set of feasible states of nature—that is, the set of possible distributions for outcomes under the innovation. Thus, learning is a process of sequential reduction in ambiguity. A question of considerable interest is to characterize the *terminal information state*. In particular, does learning eventually yield complete knowledge of response to the innovation? The answer turns out to be generically negative. That is, laissez-faire learning typically stops short of certitude.

My basic finding on treatment choice was that social learning enables successive cohorts to shrink the set of undominated actions and, in this sense, improves their decision making. I did not take a stand on how individuals choose among undominated actions. Instead, I analyzed the dynamics of learning and treatment choice supposing that they use several alternative decision criteria.

I found that the manner in which persons choose among undominated actions can substantially affect the process of social learning. If they act pessimistically, using the maximin criterion, the adoption rate of the innovation increases with time and converges gradually to a steady state that is below the optimal rate of adoption. If they act optimistically, choosing the action that maximizes the best possible rather than worst possible outcome, the adoption rate begins high and then falls quickly to a steady state that is above the optimal rate of adoption.

Laissez-Faire Learning and Adaptive Diversification

In the setting of Manski (2004b, 2005b), planning generically yields higher utilitarian welfare than does laissez-faire treatment choice. The reason is that the planner can adaptively diversify treatment, generating randomized experiments that eventually yield complete knowledge of response to the innovation. In contrast, individuals making their own treatment choices must draw inferences from observational study of the choices made and outcomes realized by previous cohorts. Not knowing the decision processes of earlier cohorts, they can only partially learn response to the innovation.

The broad lesson, in the language of public economics, is that learning is a public good. A planner has the power to undertake randomized experiments that maximize learning and that eventually enable optimal treatment choice. Individuals do not take into account the implications of their treatment choices for the knowledge possessed by future cohorts. Hence, laissez-faire yields less learning.

6

Policy Analysis and Decisions

AN IMPORTANT objective of policy analysis should be to provide information useful in making policy decisions. Part I of this book described the practice of policy analysis and the inferential problems that researchers confront. I argued that credible analysis typically yields interval rather than point predictions of policy outcomes. Part II examined how a planner or a decision group might reasonably choose policy with partial knowledge. This short closing chapter presents some ideas that tie the two parts of the book together.

Institutional Separation of Analysis and Decisions

Modern democratic societies have created an institutional separation between policy analysis and decisions, with professional analysts reporting findings to representative governments. Separation of the tasks of analysis and decision making, the former aiming to inform the latter, appears advantageous from the perspective of division of labor. No one can be expert at everything. In principle, having researchers provide outcome predictions to lawmakers and civil servants enables these decision makers to focus on the challenging task of policy choice in an uncertain world, without having to perform their own research.

However, the current practice of policy analysis does not serve decision makers well. The problem is that the consumers of policy analysis cannot trust the producers. Chapter 1 cautioned that it does not suffice to trust peer review to certify the logic or credibility of research. To mitigate the problem, I recommended that journalists reporting on

policy analysis should assess whether and how researchers express uncertainty about their findings, and should be deeply skeptical of studies
that assert certitude. This caution and advice extend to all readers of
policy analysis.

I observed in Chapter 2 that, in the absence of trust, consumers of
policy analysis need to understand prediction methods well enough to
be able to assess the credibility of reported findings. Hence, I devoted
Chapters 2 and 3 to exposition of the inferential difficulties in prediction of outcomes and the analytical approaches in common use. In the
current environment, I think it prudent for lawmakers, civil servants,
and citizens who participate in policy formation to obtain the basic understanding of policy analysis that I have endeavored to convey.

Everyone concerned with policy making should keep in mind several dangers of policy analysis with incredible certitude. First, planning
with incredible certitude seeks to maximize the social welfare that
would prevail if untenable assumptions were to hold rather than *actual*
social welfare. Second, incredible certitude prevents recognition of the
value of diversification as a means to cope with uncertainty. Third, incredible certitude inhibits performance of new research aiming to learn
about policy outcomes.

Doing Better

While I find it important to encourage skepticism of certitude and
awareness of inferential problems, I think it does not suffice. Consumers of policy analysis still face the problem of interpreting the research
findings that they receive. In Chapter 1, I gave the example of congressional staffer Scott Lilly, who told me that he found it prudent to view
all policy analysis as advocacy and that he was able to learn from studies only to the extent that he was aware of the biases of the authors. It
is good that Lilly is skeptical of reported findings, but he still must conjecture the direction and magnitude of de-biasing that each finding
warrants.

Several economists knowledgeable about CBO analysis have told
me that they are aware that scores are just estimates. Well enough, but
they still have to interpret reported scores. Should they take a CBO
point prediction to be the midpoint of an unreported credible interval
prediction? For example, should they think of the March 2010 forecast

of a $138 billion reduction in the deficit following passage of major health care legislation as the midpoint of an interval prediction with width $10 billion, $100 billion, $1,000 billion, or what?

Rather than require the consumers of policy analysis to guess how to interpret point predictions, researchers could provide credible interval predictions. I am aware that some think this idea to be naive, impractical, or worse. In Chapter 1, I quoted my econometrics colleague Jerry Hausman, who told me, "You can't give the client a bound. The client needs a point." I reported the view of former CBO director Douglas Holtz-Eakin, who told me that Congress would be highly displeased if the CBO were to provide interval scores. And I have repeatedly heard policy analysts assert that policy makers are either psychologically unwilling or cognitively unable to cope with uncertainty. The analysts who express this view tend to do so with certitude.

I do not know for sure that analysis offering credible interval predictions will lead to better policy decisions than the current practice of prediction with incredible certitude. To claim this would subject me to a charge of incredible certitude, which I certainly want to avoid. What I will suggest is application of the lessons of this book to policy analysis itself.

The current practice of point prediction constitutes a status quo treatment. Provision of credible interval predictions is an innovation. An outcome of interest is the quality of policy decisions. Society has meager knowledge of the relative merits of the status quo and the innovation. To cope with this uncertainty and to learn what type of policy analysis works best, society could use each in different settings and implement a strategy of adaptive diversification.

Appendix A
Derivations for Criteria to Treat X-Pox

Section 4.3 described policy choice when different decision criteria are used to treat x-pox. This appendix gives the derivations when there are two states of nature. Treatment A is effective in state s and treatment B in state t.

Expected Welfare: The planner places subjective probabilities on the two states of nature and evaluates a treatment allocation by its expected welfare. Suppose that he places probability p on state t and $1-p$ on state s. Then the expected welfare from assigning a fraction d of the population to B and $1-d$ to A is $p \times d + (1-p) \times (1-d)$. If p is larger than $\frac{1}{2}$, assigning everyone to treatment B maximizes expected welfare. If p is smaller than $\frac{1}{2}$, assigning everyone to A maximizes expected welfare. If p equals $\frac{1}{2}$, all treatment allocations yield the same expected welfare.

Maximin: The planner evaluates a treatment allocation by the minimum welfare that it may yield. The welfare from assigning a fraction d of the population to treatment B and $1-d$ to A is known to be either d or $1-d$. Hence, the minimum welfare from this allocation is the minimum of d and $1-d$. The allocation that maximizes minimum welfare is $d = \frac{1}{2}$. Thus, a planner using the maximin criterion assigns half of the population to each treatment.

Minimax Regret: In each state of nature, one can achieve full survival of the population by allocating everyone to the treatment that is effective in this state. Thus, the regret of a candidate treatment allocation equals one minus the survival rate achieved by this allocation. Formally, the regret from assigning a fraction d of the population to treatment B and $1-d$ to A equals d in state s and $1-d$ in state t. Hence, the maximum regret of this allocation is the maximum of d and $1-d$. The allocation that minimizes maximum regret is $d = \frac{1}{2}$. Thus, a planner using the minimax-regret criterion assigns half of the population to each treatment.

Appendix B
The Minimax-Regret Allocation to a Status Quo
Treatment and an Innovation

Section 5.1 gave the form of the minimax-regret allocation when treatment A is a status quo and B is an innovation. I prove the result here.

Consider a treatment allocation assigning a fraction d of the population to treatment B and $1-d$ to A. To determine the maximum regret of this allocation, partition the state space into two regions. One region lists the states of nature where treatment B is superior to A, and the other lists the states where A is superior to B.

In the first region of the state space, type B errors cannot occur, but a type A error occurs when a person is assigned to the status quo. The regret of allocation d in a state s where treatment B is superior to A is the welfare $W(1, s)$ that would occur if everyone were assigned to the innovation minus the welfare achieved by allocation d. Thus, regret in the first region is

$$W(1, s) - [(1-d) \times W_0 + d \times W(1, s)] = (1-d) \times [W(1, s) - W_0].$$

The maximum regret of allocation d in this region occurs when $W(1, s)$ equals its upper bound $H(1)$. Hence, the maximum regret of d in this region is $(1-d) \times [H(1) - W_0]$. Thus, maximum regret is the fraction of the population receiving treatment A multiplied by the maximum welfare loss created by this treatment assignment.

In the second region, type A errors cannot occur, but a type B error occurs when a person is assigned to the innovation. The regret of allocation d in a state s where treatment A is superior to B is the welfare W_0 that would occur if everyone were assigned to the status quo minus the welfare achieved by d. Thus, regret in this region is

$$W_0 - [(1-d) \times W_0 + d \times W(1, s)] = d \times [W_0 - W(1, s)].$$

The maximum regret of d in this region occurs when $W(1, s)$ equals its lower bound $L(1)$. Hence, the maximum regret of d in this region is $d \times [W_0 - L(1)]$. This is the fraction of the population receiving B multiplied by the maximum welfare loss created by this treatment assignment.

Combining these results shows that the overall maximum regret for allocation d is the maximum of the two quantities $(1-d) \times [H(1) - W_0]$ and $d \times [W_0 - L(1)]$. Now consider choice of d to minimize the maximum of the two quantities. The first quantity decreases with d, while the second increases with d. Hence, the minimum occurs when d equalizes the two quantities. Thus, the minimax-regret allocation solves the equation

$$(1-d) \times [H(1) - W_0] = d \times [W_0 - L(1)].$$

The value of d that solves this equation is

$$d = \frac{H(1) - W_0}{H(1) - L(1)}.$$

This allocation balances the maximum welfare losses from type A and B errors.

Appendix C
Treatment Choice with Partial Knowledge of Response
to Both Treatments

Although I have used the evocative terms *status quo* and *innovation* to distinguish treatments *A* and *B* in this chapter, these treatments differed formally not in novelty but in the planner's knowledge of treatment response. The planner knew the welfare that would occur if everyone were to receive *A*, but not the welfare that would occur if everyone were to receive *B*. Suppose now that the planner has partial knowledge of response to both treatments. Then the analysis is not as simple, but important findings can be proved. I will describe them briefly. Manski (2009) presents the full analysis.

Expected Welfare

A risk-neutral planner assigns everyone to the treatment with the higher expected mean outcome. A risk-averse planner may assign everyone to one treatment or may diversify. The specific result depends on the interplay of the planner's subjective probability distribution and welfare function.

Maximin

The maximin allocation depends on the structure of the state space. When considering allocation to a status quo treatment and an innovation, we found that the maximin criterion assigned everyone to the status quo. When considering treatment of x-pox, we found that the maximin criterion allocated half the population to each treatment when s and t were the only states of nature. However, all allocations maximized minimum welfare when a third state u was added in which

neither treatment works. These findings show that the maximin criterion may or may not yield a diversified allocation, depending on the state
space.

Recall that $L(1)$ and $H(1)$ denote the lowest and highest values that
$W(1, s)$ takes across all feasible states of nature. Let $L(0)$ and $H(0)$ similarly denote the lowest and highest values that $W(0, s)$ takes across all
feasible states. It is easy to show that the maximin criterion does not
diversify if there exists a state of nature such that welfare under treatments A and B both attain their lower bounds. That is, suppose there
exists a state s such that $W(0, s) = L(0)$ and $W(1, s) = L(1)$. Then minimum welfare under any allocation d is $(1-d){\times}L(0) + d{\times}L(1)$. Hence, the
maximin allocation is $d = 0$ if $L(0)$ exceeds $L(1)$ and is $d = 1$ if $L(1)$ exceeds $L(0)$. All allocations solve the maximin problem if $L(0) = L(1)$.

Minimax Regret

Manski (2007a, chap. 11) and Manski (2009) show that the minimax-
regret criterion always yields a diversified treatment allocation when
there is partial knowledge of response to both treatments. The general
allocation formula is too abstract to give here, but it is simple in a broad
class of problems.

Suppose that there exists a state of nature such that the welfare of
assigning everyone to treatment A achieves its upper bound and of assigning everyone to B achieves its lower bound. That is, there exists a
state s such that $W(0, s) = H(0)$ and $W(1, s) = L(1)$. Similarly, suppose that
there exists a state t such that $W(0, t) = L(0)$ and $W(1, t) = H(1)$. The planner does not know which treatment is best if $H(1) > L(0)$ and $H(0) > L(1)$.
Then the minimax-regret allocation turns out to be

$$d = \frac{H(1) - L(0)}{[H(1) - L(0)] + [H(0) - L(1)]}.$$

When $L(0) = H(0)$, this formula reduces to the one derived in our analysis of allocation to a status quo treatment and innovation.

Treatment of x-pox provides a ready illustration with partial knowledge of response to both treatments. In the x-pox scenario, there existed
a state s such that $W(0, s) = H(0) = 1$, and $W(1, s) = L(1) = 0$. There existed a
state t such that $W(0, t) = L(0) = 0$, and $W(1, t) = H(1) = 1$. The minimax-
regret allocation was $(1-0)/[(1-0) + (1-0)] = \frac{1}{2}$.

References

Angrist, J. 1990. "Lifetime Earnings and the Vietnam Era Draft Lottery: Evidence from Social Security Administrative Records." *American Economic Review* 80:313–336.

Angrist, J., G. Imbens, and D. Rubin. 1996. "Identification of Causal Effects Using Instrumental Variables." *Journal of the American Statistical Association* 91:444–455.

Angrist, J., and A. Krueger. 1991. "Does Compulsory School Attendance Affect Schooling and Earnings." *Quarterly Journal of Economics* 106:979–1014.

Applebaum, A. 2005. "The Drug Approval Pendulum." *Washington Post*, April 13, p. A17.

Arrow, K. 1951. *Social Choice and Individual Values*. New York: Wiley.

Auerbach, A. 1996. "Dynamic Revenue Estimation." *Journal of Economic Perspectives* 10:141–157.

Ball F., and O. Lyne. 2002. "Optimal Vaccination Policies for Stochastic Epidemics among a Population of Households." *Mathematical Biosciences* 177&178:333–354.

Bassi, L., and O. Ashenfelter. 1986. "The Effect of Direct Job Creation and Training Programs on Low-Skilled Workers." In *Fighting Poverty: What Works and What Doesn't*, ed. S. Danziger and D. Weinberg. Cambridge, MA: Harvard University Press.

Becker, G. 1968. "Crime and Punishment: An Economic Approach." *Journal of Political Economy* 76:169–217.

Berger J. 1985. *Statistical Decision Theory and Bayesian Analysis*. New York: Springer-Verlag.

Binmore K. 2009. *Rational Decisions*. Princeton, NJ: Princeton University Press.

Black, D. 1948. "On the Rationale of Group Decision-Making." *Journal of Political Economy* 56:23–34.

Blackmore, J., and J. Welsh. 1983. "Selective Incapacitation: Sentencing According to Risk." *Crime and Deliquency* 29:504–528.

Bloom, H. 1984. "Accounting for No-Shows in Experimental Evaluation Designs." *Evaluation Review* 8:225–246.

Blumstein, A., J. Cohen, and D. Nagin, eds. 1978. *Deterrence and Incapacitation: Estimating the Effects of Criminal Sanctions on Crime Rates.* Washington, DC: National Academy Press.

Blumstein, A., J. Cohen, J. Roth, and C. Visher, eds. 1986. *Criminal Careers and Career Criminals.* Washington, DC: National Academy Press.

Blundell, R., and T. MaCurdy. 1999. "Labor Supply: A Review of Alternative Approaches." In *Handbook of Labor Economics,* vol. 3, ed. O. Ashenfelter and D. Card, 1559–1695. Amsterdam: Elsevier.

Bork R. (solicitor general) et al. 1974. *Fowler v. North Carolina.* U.S. Supreme Court case no. 73-7031. Brief for U.S. as amicus curiae, 32–39.

Brito D., E. Sheshinski, and M. Intriligator. 1991. "Externalities and Compulsory Vaccinations." *Journal of Public Economics* 45:69–90.

Britton, E., P. Fisher, and J. Whitley. 1998. "The *Inflation Report* Projections: Understanding the Fan Chart." *Bank of England Quarterly Bulletin,* February, 30–37.

Burtless, G., and J. Hausman. 1978. "The Effect of Taxation on Labor Supply: Evaluating the Gary Negative Income Tax Experiment." *Journal of Political Economy* 86:1103–1130.

Campbell, D. 1984. "Can We Be Scientific in Applied Social Science?" *Evaluation Studies Review Annual* 9:26–48.

Campbell, D., and J. Stanley. 1963. *Experimental and Quasi-Experimental Designs for Research.* Chicago: Rand McNally.

Card, D., and A. Krueger. 1994. "Minimum Wages and Employment: A Case Study of the Fast-Food Industry in New Jersey and Pennsylvania." *American Economic Review* 84:772–793.

———. 1995. *Myth and Measurement: The New Economics of the Minimum Wage.* Princeton, NJ: Princeton University Press.

Caspi, A., et al. 2003. "Influence of Life Stress on Depression: Moderation by a Polymorphism in the 5-HTT Gene." *Science* 301:386–389.

Chaiken, J., and M. Chaiken. 1982. *Varieties of Criminal Behavior.* Report R-2814-NIJ, Santa Monica, CA: RAND Corp.

Chetty, R., J. Friedman, N. Hilger, E. Saez, D. Whitmore Schanzenbach, and D. Yagan. 2011. "How Does Your Kindergarten Classroom Affect Your Earnings? Evidence from Project Star." *Quarterly Journal of Economics* 126:1593–1660.

Committee on the Budget, U.S. House of Representatives. 2008. *Compilation of Laws and Rules Relating to the Congressional Budget Process.* Serial No. CP-3. Washington, DC: Government Printing Office.

Committee on Deterrence and the Death Penalty, National Research Council. 2012. *Deterrence and the Death Penalty.* Washington, DC: National Academies Press.

Congressional Budget Office. 1996. "Labor Supply and Taxes." Memorandum. http://www.cbo.gov/ftpdocs/33xx/doc3372/labormkts.pdf.

Congressional Budget Office. 2007. "The Effect of Tax Changes on Labor Supply in CBO's Microsimulation Tax Model." Background paper. http://www.cbo.gov/ftpdocs/79xx/doc7996/04-12-LaborSupply.pdf.

Coyle, S., R. Boruch, and C. Turner, eds. 1991. *Evaluating AIDS Prevention Programs.* Washington, DC: National Academy Press.

Crane, B, A. Rivolo, and G. Comfort. 1997. *An Empirical Examination of Counterdrug Interdiction Program Effectiveness.* IDA paper P-3219. Alexandria, VA: Institute for Defense Analyses.

Delavande, A. 2008. "Pill, Patch, or Shot? Subjective Expectations and Birth Control Choice." *International Economic Review* 49:999–1042.

Delavande, A., X. Giné, and D. McKenzie. 2011. "Measuring Subjective Expectations in Developing Countries: A Critical Review and New Evidence." *Journal of Development Economics* 94:151–163.

Department for Business, Innovation and Skills. 2011. *Impact Assessment Toolkit.* http://www.bis.gov.uk/assets/biscore/better-regulation/docs/i/11 -1112-impact-assessment-toolkit.pdf

Dominitz, J. 2003. "How Do the Laws of Probability Constrain Legislative and Judicial Efforts to Stop Racial Profiling?" *American Law and Economics Review* 5:412–432.

Dubin, J., and D. Rivers. 1993. "Experimental Estimates of the Impact of Wage Subsidies." *Journal of Econometrics* 56:219–242.

Ehrlich, I. 1975. "The Deterrent Effect of Capital Punishment: A Question of Life and Death." *American Economic Review* 65:397–417.

Ellsberg, D. 1961. "Risk, Ambiguity, and the Savage Axioms." *Quarterly Journal of Economics* 75:643–669.

Elmendorf, D. 2010a. Letter to Honorable Nancy Pelosi, Speaker, U.S. House of Representatives. Congressional Budget Office, March 18. http://www .cbo.gov/ftpdocs/113xx/doc11355/hr4872.pdf.

———. 2010b. Letter to Honorable Paul Ryan, U.S. House of Representatives. Congressional Budget Office, March 19. http://www.cbo.gov/ftpdocs /113xx/doc11376/RyanLtrhr4872.pdf.

Encyclopaedia Britannica Online. 2010. http://www.britannica.com/EBchecked /topic/424706/Ockhams-razor.

Fisher, L., and L. Moyé. 1999. "Carvedilol and the Food and Drug Administration Approval Process: An Introduction." *Controlled Clinical Trials* 20:1–15.

Fisher, R. 1935. *The Design of Experiments.* London: Oliver and Boyd.

Fishman, M., and D. Weinberg. 1992. "The Role of Evaluation in State Welfare Reform Waiver Demonstrations." In *Evaluating Welfare and Training Programs,* ed. C. Manski and I. Garfinkel, 115–142. Cambridge, MA: Harvard University Press.

Fleming, T., and D. Demets. 1996. "Surrogate End Points in Clinical Trials: Are We Being Misled?" *Annals of Internal Medicine* 125:605–613.

Foster, R. 2010. *Estimated Financial Effects of the "Patient Protection and Affordable Care Act," as Amended.* Office of the Actuary, Centers for Medicare and Medicaid Services, U.S. Department of Health and Human Services. April 22. https://www.cms.gov/ActuarialStudies/Downloads/PPACA_2010-04 -22.pdf

Friedman, M. 1953. *Essays in Positive Economics.* Chicago: University of Chicago Press.

———. 1955. "The Role of Government in Education." In *Economics and the Public Interest,* ed. R. Solo. New Brunswick, NJ: Rutgers University Press.

———. 1962. *Capitalism and Freedom.* Chicago: University of Chicago Press.

Friedman, M., and L. Savage. 1948. "The Utility Analysis of Choices Involving Risk." *Journal of Political Economy* 56:279–304.

Galbraith, J. K. 1958. *The Affluent Society.* New York: Mentor Books.

Goldberger, A. 1979. "Heritability," *Economica* 46:327–347.

Goldberger, A., and C. Manski. 1995. "Review Article: *The Bell Curve* by Herrnstein and Murray." *Journal of Economic Literature* 33:762–776.

Greenberg, D., and M. Wiseman. 1992. "What Did the OBRA Demonstrations Do?" In *Evaluating Welfare and Training Programs,* ed. C. Manski and I. Garfinkel, 25–75. Cambridge, MA: Harvard University Press.

Greenwood, P., and A. Abrahamse. 1982. *Selective Incapacitation.* Report R-2815-NIJ. Santa Monica, CA: RAND Corp.

Griliches, Z. 1957. "Hybrid Corn: An Exploration in the Economics of Technological Change." *Econometrica* 25:501–522.

Gueron, J., and E. Pauly. 1991. *From Welfare to Work.* New York: Russell Sage Foundation.

Halloran, M., I. Longini, and C. Stuchiner. 2009. *Design and Analysis of Vaccine Studies.* New York: Springer.

Harsanyi, J. 1953. "Cardinal Utility in Welfare Economics and in the Theory of Risk-Taking." *Journal of Political Economy* 61:434–435.

Hausman, J., and D. Wise, eds. 1985. *Social Experimentation.* Chicago: University of Chicago Press.

Heckman, J. 1976. "The Common Structure of Statistical Models of Truncation, Sample Selection, and Limited Dependent Variables and a Simple Estimator for Such Models." *Annals of Economic and Social Measurement* 5:479–492.

————. 1979. "Sample Selection Bias as a Specification Error." *Econometrica* 47:153–161.

Heckman, J., and C. Taber. 2008. "Roy Model." *The New Palgrave Dictionary of Economics.* 2nd ed. Ed. S. Durlauf and L. Blume. London: Palgrave Macmillan.

Herrnstein, R., and C. Murray. 1994. *The Bell Curve: Intelligence and Class Structure in American Life.* New York: Free Press.

Herszenhorn, D. 2010. "Fine-Tuning Led to Health Bill's $940 Billion Price Tag." *New York Times,* March 18.

Hill, A., and I. Longini. 2003. "The Critical Vaccination Fraction for Heterogeneous Epidemic Models." *Mathematical Biosciences* 181:85–106.

Holtz-Eakin, D. 2010. "The Real Arithmetic of Health Care Reform." *New York Times,* March 21.

Hotz, J. 1992. "Designing an Evaluation of the Job Training Partnership Act." In *Evaluating Welfare and Training Programs,* ed. C. Manski and I. Garfinkel. Cambridge, MA: Harvard University Press.

Hurd, M. 2009. "Subjective Probabilities in Household Surveys." *Annual Review of Economics* 1:543–564.

Imbens, G., and J. Angrist. 1994. "Identification and Estimation of Local Average Treatment Effects." *Econometrica* 62:467–476.

Kahneman, D., and A. Tversky. 1979. "Prospect Theory: An Analysis of Decision under Risk." *Econometrica* 47:263–291.

Keane, M. 2011. "Labor Supply and Taxes: A Survey." *Journal of Economic Literature* 49:961–1075.

Kempthorne, O. 1978. "Logical, Epistemological, and Statistical Aspects of Nature-Nurture Data Interpretation." *Biometrics* 34:1–23.

Kennan, J. 1995. "The Elusive Effects of Minimum Wages." *Journal of Economic Literature* 33:1949–1965.

Keynes J. 1921. *A Treatise on Probability.* London: Macmillan.

Killingsworth, M., and J. Heckman. 1986. "Female Labor Supply: A Survey." In *Handbook of Labor Economics,* vol. 1, ed. O. Ashenfelter and R. Layard, 103–204. Amsterdam: North-Holland.

Knight F. 1921. *Risk, Uncertainty, and Profit.* Boston: Houghton Mifflin.

Knowles, J., N. Persico, and P. Todd. 2001. "Racial Bias in Motor Vehicle Searches: Theory and Evidence." *Journal of Political Economy* 109:203–229.

Krugman, P. 2007. "Who Was Milton Friedman?" *New York Review of Books,* February 15.

Kühberger, A. 2002. "The Rationality of Risky Decisions." *Theory and Psychology* 12:427–452.

LaLonde, R. 1986. "Evaluating the Econometric Evaluations of Training Programs with Experimental Data." *American Economic Review* 76:604–620.

Lopes, L. 1991. "The Rhetoric of Irrationality." *Theory and Psychology* 1:65–82.

Luce, R., and P. Suppes. 1965. "Preference, Utility, and Subjective Probability."
In *Handbook of Mathematical Psychology,* vol. 3, ed. R. Luce, R. Bush, and
E. Galanter. New York: Wiley.

Maddala, G. S. 1983. *Limited-Dependent and Qualitative Variables in Econometrics.*
Cambridge: Cambridge University Press.

Manski C. 1990. "Nonparametric Bounds on Treatment Effects." *American
Economic Review Papers and Proceedings* 80:319–323.

————. 1992. "School *Choice* (Vouchers) and Social Mobility." *Economics of
Education Review* 11:351–369.

————. 1993. "Adolescent Econometricians: How Do Youth Infer the Returns
to Schooling?" In *Studies of Supply and Demand in Higher Education,* ed.
C. Clotfelter and M. Rothschild, 43–57. Chicago: University of
Chicago Press.

————. 1995. *Identification Problems in the Social Sciences.* Cambridge, MA:
Harvard University Press.

————. 1997a. "The Mixing Problem in Programme Evaluation." *Review of
Economic Studies* 64:537–553.

————. 1997b. "Monotone Treatment Response." *Econometrica* 65:1311–1334.

————. 2003. *Partial Identification of Probability Distributions.* New York:
Springer-Verlag.

————. 2004a. "Measuring Expectations." *Econometrica* 72:1329–1376.

————. 2004b. "Social Learning from Private Experiences: The Dynamics of
the Selection Problem." *Review of Economic Studies* 71:443–458.

————. 2005a. *Social Choice with Partial Knowledge of Treatment Response.*
Princeton, NJ: Princeton University Press.

————. 2005b. "Social Learning and the Adoption of Innovations." In *The
Economy as an Evolving Complex System III,* ed. L. Blume and S. Durlauf.
Oxford: Oxford University Press.

————. 2006. "Search Profiling with Partial Knowledge of Deterrence."
Economic Journal 116:F385–F401.

————. 2007a. *Identification for Prediction and Decision.* Cambridge, MA:
Harvard University Press.

————. 2007b. "Partial Identification of Counterfactual Choice Probabilities."
International Economic Review 48:1393–1410.

————. 2009. "Diversified Treatment under Ambiguity." *International Economic
Review* 50:1013–1041.

————. 2010. "Vaccination with Partial Knowledge of External Effectiveness."
Proceedings of the National Academy of Sciences 107:3953–3960.

————. 2011a. "Choosing Treatment Policies under Ambiguity." *Annual Review
of Economics* 3:25–49.

————. 2011b. "Policy Analysis with Incredible Certitude." *Economic Journal*
121:F261–F289.

———. 2011c. "Genes, Eyeglasses, and Social Policy." *Journal of Economic Perspectives* 25:83–94.

———. 2011d. "Actualist Rationality." *Theory and Decision* 71:195–210.

———. 2012. "Identification of Preferences and Evaluation of Income Tax Policy." National Bureau of Economic Research Working Paper w17755.

Manski, C., and I. Garfinkel, eds. 1992. *Evaluating Welfare and Training Programs.* Cambridge, MA: Harvard University Press.

Manski, C., and D. Nagin. 1998. "Bounding Disagreements about Treatment Effects: A Case Study of Sentencing and Recidivism." *Sociological Methodology* 28:99–137.

Manski, C., and J. Pepper. 2012. "Deterrence and the Death Penalty: Partial Identification Analysis Using Repeated Cross Sections." *Journal of Quantitative Criminology,* forthcoming.

Manski, C., and D. Wise. 1983. *College Choice in America.* Cambridge, MA: Harvard University Press.

McFadden, D. 1974. "Conditional Logit Analysis of Qualitative Choice Behavior." In *Frontiers in Econometrics,* ed. P. Zarembka. New York: Academic Press.

Medina, J. 2008. "New York Measuring Teachers by Test Score." *New York Times,* January 21.

Meghir, C., and D. Phillips. 2010. "Labour Supply and Taxes." In *Dimensions of Tax Design: The Mirrlees Review,* ed. T. Besley, R. Blundell, M. Gammie, and J. Poterba, 202–274. Oxford: Oxford University Press.

Mirrlees J. 1971. "An Exploration in the Theory of Optimal Income Taxation." *Review of Economic Studies* 38:175–208.

National Research Council. 1999. *Assessment of Two Cost-Effectiveness Studies on Cocaine Control Policy.* Committee on Data and Research for Policy on Illegal Drugs. Ed. C. F. Manski, J. V. Pepper, and Y. Thomas. Committee on Law and Justice and Committee on National Statistics, Commission on Behavioral and Social Sciences and Education. Washington, DC: National Academy Press.

———. 2001. *Informing America's Policy on Illegal Drugs: What We Don't Know Keeps Hurting Us.* Committee on Data and Research for Policy on Illegal Drugs. Ed. C. F. Manski, J. V. Pepper, and C. V. Petrie. Committee on Law and Justice and Committee on National Statistics, Commission on Behavioral and Social Sciences and Education. Washington, DC: National Academy Press.

Page, R. 2005. "CBO's Analysis of the Macroeconomic Effects of the President's Budget." *American Economic Review Papers and Proceedings* 95:437–440.

Patel R., I. Longini, and E. Halloran. 2005. "Finding Optimal Vaccination Strategies for Pandemic Influenza Using Genetic Algorithms." *Journal of Theoretical Biology* 234:201–212.

Pencavel, J. 1986. "Labor Supply of Men: A Survey." In *Handbook of Labor Economics*, vol. 1, ed. O. Ashenfelter and R. Layard, 3–102. Amsterdam: North-Holland.

Persico, N. 2002. "Racial Profiling, Fairness, and the Effectiveness of Policing." *American Economic Review* 92:1472–1497.

Psaty, B. et al. 1999. "Surrogate End Points, Health Outcomes, and the Drug-Approval Process for the Treatment of Risk Factors for Cardiovascular Disease." *Journal of the American Medical Association* 282:786–790.

Rawls, J. 1971. *A Theory of Justice.* Cambridge, MA: Belknap Press of Harvard University Press.

Robbins, L. 1930. "On the Elasticity of Demand for Income in Terms of Effort." *Economica* 29:123–129.

Roosevelt, T. 1912. Introduction to C. McCarthy, *The Wisconsin Idea*. New York: McMillan.

Rosenbaum, P. 1999. "Choice as an Alternative to Control in Observational Studies." *Statistical Science* 14:259–304.

Roy, A. 1951. "Some Thoughts on the Distribution of Earnings." *Oxford Economic Papers* 3:135–146.

Rumsfeld, D. 2001. "Rumsfeld's Rules." *Wall Street Journal,* January 29.

———. 2002. Statement made in a radio interview for Infinity Broadcasting, quoted by CNN on November 15. http://archives.cnn.com/2002/US/11/15/rumsfeld.iraq/index.html.

Rydell, C., and S. Everingham. 1994. *Controlling Cocaine.* Report prepared for the Office of National Drug Control Policy and the U.S. Army. Santa Monica, CA: RAND Corp.

Saez, E., J. Slemrod, and S. Giertz. 2012. "The Elasticity of Taxable Income with Respect to Marginal Tax Rates: A Critical Review." *Journal of Economic Literature,* 50: 3–50.

Samuelson, P. 1938. "A Note on the Pure Theory of Consumer Behavior." *Economica* 5:61–71.

———. 1948. "Consumption Theory in Terms of Revealed Preferences." *Economica* 15:243–253.

Savage L. 1951. "The Theory of Statistical Decision." *Journal of the American Statistical Association* 46:55–67.

———. 1954. *The Foundations of Statistics.* New York: Wiley.

Shanteau, J. 1989. "Cognitive Heuristics and Biases in Behavioral Auditing: Review, Comments, and Observations." *Accounting, Organizations and Society* 14:165–177.

Simon, H. 1955. "A Behavioral Model of Rational Choice." *Quarterly Journal of Economics* 69:99–118.

Smith, D., and R. Paternoster. 1990. "Formal Processing and Future Delinquency: Deviance Amplification as Selection Artifact." *Law and Society Review* 24:1109–1131.

Stanovich, K., and R. West. 2000. "Individual Differences in Reasoning: Implications for the Rationality Debate?" *Behavioral and Brain Sciences* 23:645–726.

Stern, N. 1986. "On the Specification of Labour Supply Functions." In *Unemployment, Search and Labour Supply,* ed. R. Blundell and I. Walker, 143–189. Cambridge: Cambridge University Press.

Subcommittee on National Security, International Affairs, and Criminal Justice. 1996. *Hearing before the Committee on Governmental Reform and Oversight.* U.S. House of Representatives. Washington, DC: Government Printing Office.

———. 1998. *Hearing before the Committee on Governmental Reform and Oversight.* U.S. House of Representatives. Washington, DC: Government Printing Office.

Swinburne, R. 1997. *Simplicity as Evidence for Truth.* Milwaukee: Marquette University Press.

Thistlethwaite, D., and D. Campbell. 1960. "Regression-Discontinuity Analysis: An Alternative to the Ex-Post Facto Experiment." *Journal of Educational Psychology* 51:309–317.

Thurstone, L. 1927. "A Law of Comparative Judgment." *Psychological Review* 34:273–286.

Tversky, A., and D. Kahneman. 1974. "Judgment under Uncertainty: Heuristics and Biases." *Science* 185:1124–1131.

———. 1981. "The Framing of Decisions and the Psychology of Choice." *Science* 211:453–458.

———. 1986. "Rational Choice and the Framing of Decisions." *Journal of Business* 59:S251–S278.

U.S. Department of Defense. 2002. News transcript, February 12. http://www.defense.gov/transcripts/transcript.aspx?transcriptid=2636.

U.S. General Accounting Office. 1992. *Unemployed Parents.* GAO/PEMD-92-19BR, Gaithersburg, MD: U.S. General Accounting Office.

Wald A. 1950. *Statistical Decision Functions.* New York: Wiley.

Wikipedia. 2010. http://en.wikipedia.org/wiki/Conventional_wisdom (accessed May 8, 2010).

Woodbury, S., and R. Spiegelman. 1987. "Bonuses to Workers and Employers to Reduce Unemployment: Randomized Trials in Illinois." *American Economic Review* 77:513–530.

Index

A and B treatment: predicting outcomes and, 47, 50–51, 54–59, 60–61, 65–67; treatment choice and, 141–148
Abrahamse, A., 31
actualist rationality, 134–135
adaptive diversification, 6, 150–154, 156–160, 172
adaptive minimax-regret criterion (AMR), 151–154, *152*, 158–159
additive preference type, 87–88
advocacy and science, 27–30
ambiguity, 122–124, 136–137
American Progressive movement, 155
AMR. *See* adaptive minimax-regret criterion (AMR)
analysis: logic and credibility of, 11–13; decisions and, 173–175; with incredible certitude (*see* certitude(s)); predictions and (*see* predictions of behavior; predictions of policy outcomes)
Angrist, J., 36–37, 80–81
Applebaum, Anne, 157
Arrow, K., 160–162
Ashenfelter, O., 67, 84
as-if rationality, 103–105
assumption(s): strong, 4–5, 11–12, 13, 47; identical-response, 5, 59–63, 65, 77; weak, 5, 47, 64; *nonrefutable*, 12–13; PPACA and, 23; illegal drug policy reports and, 24–27; predetermined conclusions and, 27–28; extrapolation and, 31; *invariance*, 31–32, 33–34; individualistic treatment response and,

32–35, 52, 56–57, 74–76; death penalty studies and, 50–51; recidivism and, 55–57; point predictions and, 59; compliance and, 69–70; perfect foresight as, 78–79, 99; distributional, 83–84; revealed preference analysis and, 85–86, 98; of economists, 89–90, 99, 102–105; rational expectations and, 99–101; utility function/maximization theory and, 100–101; welfare function and, 119–121
attribute representation, 94–95
Auerbach, Alan, 17, 21
axiomatic decision theory, 133–138
axiomatic rationality, 134–135

Ball, F., 129
Bank of England, 22–23
Barnhart, Jo Anne, 67, 68
Bassi, L., 67, 84
Bayesian decision theory, 122, 136
Bayes Theorem, 107
Becker, Gary, 100
before-and-after analysis, 50–51, 60–61
behavior. *See* predictions of behavior
behavioral economics, 103, 105
Bell Curve, The (Herrnstein and Murray), 40, 42
Berger, James, 136
bias: selection, 78–79; and heuristics, 106–110
bilateral negotiations, 166–169
Binmore, K., 135

Black, D., 162
Blackmore, J., 32
Bloom, H., 36
Blumstein, A., 32, 48
Blundell, R., 90
Bork, R., 48
Boruch, R., 67
bounded rationality, 105–106
bounds. *See* interval predictions (bounds)
Brandeis, Louis, 155
British norms, conventional certitudes
    and, 22–23
Brito, D., 129
Brown, Lee, 25
brutalization effect, 51
Burtless, G., 90

Campbell, Donald, 36–37, 76, 80, 81
capital punishment. *See* death penalty
Card, David, 61–63
Caspi, A., 43
certitude(s), 4, 11–46; strong assumptions
    and, 11–12; logic, credibility and,
    11–13; incentives for, 13–15; conven-
    tional, 15–23; dueling, 23–27, 86–93,
    110–111; science conflated with
    advocacy and, 27–30; wishful extrapo-
    lation and, 30–37; illogical, 37–43;
    media overreach and, 44–46; econo-
    mists and, 81–82; quest for rationality
    and, 137–138; assessing, 173–175;
    dangers of, 174
Chaiken, J. and M., 31
Chetty, Raj, 44–45
choice, rational, 99
choice probabilities, 94–95
choice sets, 85–86
classical experiments, 65–66, 73, 76
clinical equipoise, 149
clinical trials. *See* randomized clinical
    trials (RCTs)
Cobb-Douglas preference type, 87–88
Cohen, J., 48
cohort, diversification by, 154
collective decision processes, 160–169;
    majority-rule voting and, 161–163;
    strategic interactions and, 163–164;
    learning and, 164–165; bilateral
    negotiations and, 166–169
college choice, 95–98, *97*
Comfort, G., 24, 60

Committee on the Budget (U.S. House of
    Representatives), 20–21
compliance with assigned treatments,
    69–71
conclusions: in policy analysis, 11–12;
    strong, 13, 47; predetermined, 27–28
conditional logit model, 95–98, *97*, 102
Condorcet's paradox, 161
Congress and uncertainty, 22
Congressional Budget Act, 20
Congressional Budget Office (CBO):
    scoring of, 16–22; tax policy and,
    90–91; point predictions and, 174–175
consensus, 12, 160, 165
consequentialism, 135, 148, 150, 151
consistency axioms, 132–138
contraception behavior, 102
controlled experiments, 59
conventional certitudes, 15–23, 35
counterfactual outcomes, 5, 48, 53–54,
    58, 100
covariates, 77–81, 83
Coyle, S., 67
Crane, B., 24, 60
credibility: logic and, 11–13; law of
    decreasing, 12; conventional certitude
    and, 15–23; dueling certitudes and,
    23–27, 86–93, 110–111; conflating
    science and advocacy and, 27–30;
    wishful extrapolation and, 30–37;
    illogical certitude and, 37–43; media
    overreach and, 44–45; peer review
    and, 45–46
criminal behavior study (RAND), 31–32

death penalty, 12–13, 48–51, 60
decision criteria, 121–125, 131–132; X-Pox
    treatment and, 124–125, 177–178;
    treatment choice and, 141–148,
    179–180, 181–182
decision making: reasonable, 131–132,
    138; rationality and, 131–138; collec-
    tive processes and, 160–169. *See also*
    diversified treatment choice; planners/
    planning
decision theory: elements of, 116–121;
    axiomatic, 133–138
Delavande, A., 102
Demets, D., 35, 154
deontological ethics, 135, 148, 150
deterrence, 48–51, 125–127

deviance, juvenile, 54–55

difference-in-difference (DID) studies, 51, 61–63

discrete choice analysis, 93–98

distribution of treatment response, 63–65, 68; Perry Preschool project and, 72–74; treatment choice and, 77–80; assumptions and, 83–84

diversification: adaptive, 6, 150–160, 172; financial, 139, 146; advantages of, 139–140; learning and, 140, 151, 155; profiling *vs.*, 140–141; by cohort, 154

diversified treatment choice, 6, 139–172; decision criterion and, 141–148, 179–180, 181–182; equal treatment of equals and, 148–150; AMR and, 150–154; across time or space, 154–156; adaptive partial drug approval and, 156–160; collective decision processes and, 160–169; laissez-faire and, 169–172

dominated actions, 121, 126

Dominitz, J., 125

drugs: policy on illegal, 24–27; FDA approval process for, 32–35, 52–53, 66, 68, 156–157; partial approval of, 156–160

Dubin, J., 36, 71

dueling certitudes, 23–27, 86–93, 110–111

economics/economists: certitude and, 81–82; point predictions and, 83–84; revealed preference analysis and, 85–86, 89–90; assumptions of, 89–90, 99, 102–105; discrete choice analysis and, 93–98; behavioral, 103, 105; welfare function and, 118–121; public, 119–120, 148, 150

educational vouchers, 28–30

Education Sciences Reform Act (2002), 37

Ehrlich, Isaac, 48

Ellsberg, Daniel, 123, 136–137

Elmendorf, Douglas, 17–19

empirical analysis, 88–91, 101–102, 106–109

employment and minimum wage, 61–63

environmental factors, 39–43

equal treatment of equals, 148–150

ethical principles, 148–150

Everingham, S., 24

ex ante and ex post equal treatment, 148–150

exclusion restrictions, 56

expectations: measuring, 14, 101–102; rational, 99–102

expected utility theory, 99–104, 107–108, 122, 147

expected welfare criterion, 122–125, 132, 177; treatment choice and, 142, 144, 145, 146; partial knowledge and, 181

external effectiveness, 34, 128–131

external validity, 36–37, 76, 109

extrapolation, 30–37; selective incapacitation and, 31–32; FDA drug approval process and, 32–35; internal *vs.* external validity and, 36–37; randomized experiments and, 68–69, 72–74; college choice and, 98; Kahneman and Tversky and, 109–110; federalism and, 155

Eysenck, Hans, 41

FDA (Food and Drug Administration): drug approval process of, 32–35, 52–53, 66, 68, 156–157; partial approval/licensing proposals for, 158–160

federalism, 154–156

Fisher, L., 66

Fisher, R. A., 65

Fishman M., 156

Fleming, T., 35, 154

Food, Drug, and Cosmetics Act (1938), 156

Food and Drug Administration. *See* FDA (Food and Drug Administration)

Foundations of Statistics (Savage), 132

framing in experiments, 107–108, 109, 110

Friedman, Milton: certitude and, 14–15; educational vouchers and, 28–30; as-if rationality and, 103–105

Furman v. Georgia, 49

Galbraith, John Kenneth, 15–16

Galton, Francis, 38

game theory, 166

Garfinkel, I., 67, 76

gene measurement, 43

genetic factors, 39–43

Giertz, S., 90

Giné, X., 102

global *vs.* local interactions, 75, 128
Goldberger, A., 38–42
Greenwood, P., 31–32, 156
Gregg v. Georgia, 49
Griliches, Z., 171
Gueron, J., 36, 37

Halloran, E., 127
Harsanyi, J., 165
Hausman, Jerry, 14, 66, 76, 90, 175
Heckman, J., 78–79, 83, 90
heritability, 38–43
Herrnstein, R., 40–41, 42
Herszenhorn, D., 18
heuristics, bias and, 106–110
HHS, 19
Hill, A., 129
Holloran, E., 127
Holtz-Eakin, Douglas, 22, 23, 175
homicide rates, 49–51, *50*, 61, 65
Hotz, J., 68
Hurd, M., 102

IDA. *See* Institute for Defense Analyses
    (IDA)
Identical response, 5, 59–67, 77
identical treatment: units, 5, 59–63;
    groups, 63–67
identification analysis, 52–53
illegal drug policy studies, 24–27
Illinois Unemployment Insurance
    Experiment, 69–71
illogical certitude, 37–43
Imbens, G., 37
Impact Assessment Toolkit, 23
impossibility theorem, 160–162
incentive-compatible processes, 167, 169
incentives, certitude and, 13–15, 17
income tax and labor supply, 86–93
incredible certitude. *See* certitude(s)
individualistic treatment response, 32–35,
    52, 56–57, 74–76
inference, 11–12, 52–53, 109–110, 174
Institute for Defense Analyses (IDA),
    illegal drug policy study of, 24–27, 60
intention-to-treat, 71
internal effectiveness, 34, 128–130
internal validity, 36–37
interval predictions (bounds), 3, 4, 20–22,
    55, 57–58, 175
Intriligator, M., 129

investing, risk and, 139, 146
IQ, heritability and, 38–40

Job Training Partnership Act (JTPA)
    evaluation, 66–67, 68
Johnson, Lyndon B., 13
Joint Committee on Taxation (JCT), 17
judicial decision making, 55
juvenile offenders, 54–55, 145–146

Kahneman, Daniel, 106–111, 136
Keane, M., 90–91
Kempthorne, Oscar, 42
Kennan, J., 63
Keynes, J., 123
Killingsworth, M., 90
kindergarten teachers, value of, 44–45
Knight, F., 123
Knowles, J., 125–126
Krueger, A., 61–63, 80–81
Krugman, P., 28

laboratories of democracy, 155
labor supply: income tax and, 86–93;
    theory of, 87–88; backward bending,
    88; empirical analysis of, 88–91
Laffer, Arthur, 86–87
La Follette, Robert, 155
laissez-faire treatment choice, 169–172
Lalonde, R., 67, 84
Law of Decreasing Credibility, 12
learning: diversification and, 140, 151,
    155; collective decision processes and,
    164–165, 167; from private experience,
    170–172
Leonhardt, David, 44–45
Leontief preference type, 87–88
licensing, partial, FDA and, 159–160
Lilly, Scott, 28, 174
logic of policy analysis, 11–13
Longini, I., 127, 129
Luce R., 94
Lynne, O, 129

MaCurdy, T., 90
majority-rule voting, 161–163
Manski, C.: incredible certitude and, 12,
    13, 30, 31, 40, 43; deterrence and, 49,
    61; recidivism and sentencing and,
    54–55, 82–83, 145–146; JTPA experi-
    ments and, 67, 76; compliance and, 69;

mixing problem and, 72; revealed preference analysis and, 91–93, *92;* college choice and, 95–98; measuring expectations and, 102; rational choice and, 103; partial knowledge and, 125–131, 135; treatment choice and, 139, 147, 167, 170–172, 181–182; welfare function and, 150

maximin criteria, 123–125, 126, 131–132; treatment choice and, 142, 144–148; FDA approval process and, 158; X-Pox treatment and, 177; partial knowledge and, 181–182

McFadden, Daniel, 93–95, 98

McKenzie, D., 102

median-voter theorem, 162–163

media overreach, 44–46

medical model of deviance, 54–55

Meghir, C., 90–91

minimax criteria, 132

minimax-regret criteria, 123–125, 126, 132; treatment choice and, 142, 144–146, 147, 179–180; adaptive (AMR), 151–154, *152,* 158–159; X-Pox treatment and, 177–178; partial knowledge and, 182

minimum wage, employment and, 61–63

Mirrlees, James, 120–121

mixing problem, 72–74

monotone treatment response, 130–131

Moyé, L., 66

Murray, C., 40–41, 42

Myths and Measurement: The New Economics of Minimum Wage (Card and Krueger), 62–63

Nagin, D., 48, 54–55, 82–83, 145–146

National Research Council (NRC): illegal drug policy studies and, 26–27, 60–61; deterrence and death penalty and, 48–49, 101; AIDS prevention programs and, 67

New York State Ice Co. v. Liebmann, 155

New York Times, 44–45, 168

non sequitur(s), 38–43

null hypotheses, non-rejection and, 38

observational studies, 36, 48, 55, 65, 67, 77–81

offense function, 125–126

outcome optimization model, 55–56, 78–79, 82–83

outcomes: surrogate, 34–35, 68; heritability and, 39–43. *See also* counterfactual outcomes; predictions of policy outcomes

Page, Benjamin, 20

Paine, Thomas, 28

Pareto optimality, 166–167

partial knowledge, 3, 6, 115–138; decision theory/criteria and, 116–125; search profiling and, 125–127; vaccination and, 127–131; rational and reasonable decision making and, 131–138. *See also* diversified treatment choice

Patel, R., 127

Paternoster, R., 78

Patient Protection and Affordable Care Act (PPACA) (2010), 17–19, 23

Pauly, E., 36, 37

peer review, 45–46

Pell Grant program, 95, 96–98, *97*

Pelosi, Nancy, 17–19

Pencavel, J., 90

Pepper, J., 49, 61

perfect foresight, 78–79, 99

Perry Preschool Project, 66, 72–74

Persico, N., 125–127

Phillips, D., 90–91

planners/planning, 6, 115–138; decision theory/criteria and, 116–125; search profiling and, 125–127; vaccination and, 127–131; rational and reasonable decision making and, 131–138; sequential, 140, 141, 150–151, 154; risk-averse and risk-neutral, 146–148; collective decision processes and, 160–169; laissez-faire as alternative to, 169–172. *See also* diversified treatment choice

point predictions, 4, 14, 16; CBO and, 19–21, 174–175; recidivism and, 57; assumptions and, 59; economists and, 83–84, 89

populations of interest, 33–34, 52

PPACA (Patient Protection and Affordable Care Act), 17–19, 23

preconceptions. *See* conclusions, predetermined

predictions of behavior, 85–111; income tax and labor supply and, 86–93; discrete choice analysis and, 93–98; uncertainty and, 99–102; rational choice and, 102–111
predictions of policy outcomes, 5–6, 47–84; deterrence and, 48–51; treatment response and, 51–53; treatment mandates and, 53–59; identical treatment units and, 59–63; identical treatment groups and, 63–67; randomized experiments and, 63–76; treatment choice (random) and, 77–81; treatment choice (rational) and, 78–79, 81–84; interval (bound) (*see* interval predictions); point (*see* point predictions)
Preschool Project (Perry), 66, 72–74
prisoner's dilemma (game theory), 166
probabilities: choice, 94–95; experimental psychology and, 107–108; subjective (*See* subjective probabilities)
profiling: policy, 125–127; *vs.* diversification, 140–141
progressive and proportional taxes, *92,* 92–93
prospect theory, 107–109
Psaty, B., 154
psychology, experimental, 106–109
public economics, 119–120, 148, 150
Pure Food and Drug Act (1906), 156

RAND: illegal drug policy study of, 24–27; criminal behavior study of, 31–32
randomized clinical trials (RCTs), 33–35, 66, 153–154, 156–157, 159–160
randomized experiments: extrapolation and, 32–37; assignment and, 65–66; as "gold standard," 66–67, 76; in practice, 67–76; mixing problem and, 72–74; treatment diversification and, 149, 151, 153–154
random utility model of behavior, 93–98, 97
rational choice(s), 99; treatment and, 78, 80–84; utility function/maximization and, 100–101; perspectives on, 102–111; invariance tenet of, 108–109
Rational Decisions (Binmore), 135
rational expectations, 99–102

rationality: bounded, 105–106; decision making and, 131–138; axiomatic *vs.* actualist, 134–135
Rawls, J., 165
RCTs. *See* randomized clinical trials (RCTs)
reasonable decision making, 131–132, 138
recidivism, 54–59, 82–83
Reconciliation Act (2010), 17
redistribution, 119–120
reference groups, 75
regression discontinuity analysis, 79–81
representation theorem, 133
response. *See* treatment response
returns to schooling, 100
revealed preference analysis, 5–6, 85–93
Rights of Man, The (Paine), 28
risk-averse and risk-neutral planning, 146–148
Rivers, D., 37, 71
Rivolo, A., 24, 60
Robbins, Lionel, 88
Roosevelt, Theodore, 155
Rosenbaum, Paul, 36
Roy, A. D., 79
Rubin, D., 37
Rumsfeld, Donald, 1–2, 118
Ryan, Paul, 18–19
Rydell, C., 24

Saez, E., 90
Samuelson, Paul, 86, 89
satisficing, 105
Savage, Leonard: as-if approximations and, 103–105; rationality and, 132–134, 136, 137–138
science and advocacy, 27–30
scoring (CBO), 16–22
search profiling, 125–127
"secondary deviance" hypothesis, 55
selection bias, 78–79
selection models, 82, 83
selective incapacitation, 31–32
sentencing, 54–59, 82–83, 145–146
sequential planning, 140, 141, 150–151, 154
Sheshinski, E., 129
Simon, H., 105–106, 108, 111
single-peaked preferences, 161–163
skimming model, 55–56

Slemrod, J., 90
Smith, D., 78
social choice theorists, 161, 162, 166
social interactions: and treatment response, 52, 74–76; local and global, 75, 128; collective decision processes and, 163–164
social learning. *See* learning
Spiegelman, R., 71
Stanley, J., 36, 76
states as laboratories, 154–156
states of nature, 117–118, 122
state space, 117–118
Statistical Decision Functions (Wald), 132
statistical inference, 52–53
Stern, N., 88
strategic interactions, 163–164
study populations, 33–34, 36–37, 52, 68, 77
subjective probabilities, 99, 101; expected welfare criterion and, 122, 124; consistency axioms and, 132, 135–137; treatment choice and, 144, 147
Suppes, P., 94
"supply-side" economics, 86–87
Swinburne, Richard, 15

Taber, C., 79
taxes, progressive and proportional, 92, 92–93
tax revenues, CBO scoring and, 17
teacher evaluation (NYC), 167–169
Thistlethwaite, D., 80, 81
Thurstone, L., 94
Times of London, 41, 45
Todd, P., 125–126
trade-offs, economics and, 150
transitivity, 133–134
treatment choice: random, 77–81; rational, 78–79, 81–84; diversified (*see* diversified treatment choice)
treatment groups, 63–67
treatment mandates, 53–59
treatment response: analysis of, 5, 51–53; individualistic, 32–35, 52, 56–57; internal *vs.* external validity of, 36; social interactions and, 52, 74–76; identical, 59–63; distribution of, 63–65;

77–78; groups and, 63–67; normal-linear model of, 83–84; monotone, 130–131
treatments, experimental, 34, 65–66, 69–71
treatment units, 51–52, 59–64, 75
trials, clinical. *See* randomized clinical trials (RCTs)
Turner, C., 67
Tversky, Amos, 106–111, 136

uncertainty: policy makers and, 14, 17–19, 22–23, 58, 174–175; predicting behavior under, 99–102
unemployment insurance (UI) study, 69–71
unknown unknowns, 2, 118
U.S, Department of Health and Human Services (HHS), 19
utility function/maximization theory, 87–88, 89, 91; discrete choice analysis and, 93–95, 96; assumptions and, 99, 100–101; Friedman and Savage on, 103–104; experimental psychology and, 107–108; welfare function and, 117–121

vaccination, 34, 52, 127–131
veil of ignorance, 165

Wald, Abraham, 131–132
Weinberg, D., 156
Weingarten, Randi, 168
welfare function theory, 117–119; in taxation study, 119–121; search profiling and, 126–127; vaccination and, 129; treatment choice and, 142–143, 147, 150; collective decision processes and, 165. *See also* expected welfare criterion
Welsh, J., 32
Wise, David, 66, 76, 95–98
Wiseman M., 156
Woodbury, S., 71

X-Pox treatment, 116–117, 121–125, 141, 147, 148–149, 177–178

Zeliff, William, 25